CAMBRIDGE POETRY WORKSHOP
14+

Lynn and Jeffrey Wood

CAMBRIDGE UNIVERSITY PRESS

To

Benjamin · Kate · Thomas · Elizabeth

Authors' acknowledgements

The encouragement, suggestions and constructive criticism of many colleagues and the responses of our students to these units as they were being written have helped make this book what it is. We wish particularly to thank Jill Rendell for her unflagging service at the wordprocessor, and Keith Rose of CUP and Katherine James for their painstaking attention to detail as well as for numerous wise suggestions about where this sentence could be less opaque, that assignment more lively. The shortcomings which remain are ours alone.

CONTENTS

THE POETS

William Shakespeare	1564–1616	Dylan Thomas	1914–1953
William Blake	1757–1827	Edwin Morgan	1920–
Samuel Taylor Coleridge	1772–1834	Dannie Abse	1923–
Percy Bysshe Shelley	1792–1822	Miroslav Holub	1923–
John Keats	1795–1821	Peter Appleton	1925–
Thomas Hood	1799–1845	Thom Gunn	1929–
Alfred, Lord Tennyson	1809–1892	Tony Connor	1930–
Gerard Manley Hopkins	1844–1889	Ted Hughes	1930–
Edgar Lee Masters	?1868–1950	Jenny Joseph	1932–
Laurence Binyon	1869–1945	Adrian Mitchell	1932–
Wilfred Wilson Gibson	1878–1962	Sylvia Plath	1932–1963
Alfred Noyes	1880–1959	B.S. Johnson	1933–1973
D.H. Lawrence	1885–1930	Jon Stallworthy	1935–
Ezra Pound	1885–1972	Seamus Heaney	1939–
Rupert Brooke	1887–1915	Bob Dylan	1941–
Richard Aldington	1892–1962	Ewan McColl	
Wilfred Owen	1893–1918	Vicki Feaver	1943–
Bertolt Brecht	1898–1956	Pauline Kirk	

To the Teacher

In *Cambridge Poetry Workshop* we have set out to provide a significant classroom resource: a substantial number of self-contained teaching units, each of which presents a major poem (or poems) and then leads, through individual or group explorations of the poem's themes and language, to a variety of creative and critical activities accessible to the full range of students. The units in the present volume, designed for the Third Year of the secondary school, include assignments intended to help lay the foundations for GCSE English and English Literature.

The units may be used as they stand but they are not intended to be 'teacher-proof'. Many ways will suggest themselves to you in which units may be adapted, modified and extended, and many of the strategies we suggest for particular poems will be equally successful with others. What we hope will be useful is a strong framework with a variety of tried and tested assignments. All of the material in this book has been used successfully with students in very different schools and in a variety of teaching situations.

Most of the units are appropriate for individual and small group study but they can also be used for whole class work, the teacher using the questions to initiate and develop discussion, as starting points for exploring both the text and the experience that the poem dramatises.

Strategy

As a rule, each unit consists of the following: a preamble, mapping the themes and/or emotional territory of the poem; the text (with full glossary); a number of Thinking/Talking Points which encourage close study of the poem; and a choice of creative and critical Assignments.

English teaching is often most exciting when it is most opportunist, free to respond to the direction that a discussion or an assignment takes. Wherever possible it is best to allow group work to develop at its own pace and in its own directions. If our experience is typical, as students become more confident about exploring their own experiences and concerns, a preamble will often develop a life of its own, seemingly independent of the poem to which it leads. After such creative explorations, however, what we usually find is that having studied and talked about the poem, critical work often shows an attention to and understanding of subtle points of poetic technique which is much more confident, searching and lively than a conventional lit. crit. approach would have produced.

But, equally often, it can be helpful to have a framework to fall back upon, a structure of leading questions to work through which rescue discussion from circularity, and a range of clearly structured activities with sufficient variety and choice of appeal to a wide cross-section of students. It is not always easy to invent such activities 'on the hoof' and while we hope we have avoided a prescriptive approach to the study of poetry, we have certainly tried to avoid vagueness. 'Write about the poem in any way you like' is not a very helpful instruction to students who have limited literary experience.

Preliminaries: the preambles

One characteristic of poetry is *intensity* – language charged with meaning in the exploration of powerful human experiences. But that very intensity is something a listener/reader needs to be prepared for. It is disconcerting to enter a room to find somebody in a rapture of delight or overcome with grief or perplexity. There are many reasons why adolescents register discomfort about poetry. Surely one of them is simply embarrassment and confusion on encountering an inexplicable outpouring of joy or desolation.

We feel that 'the emotional territory' of a poem usually needs to be mapped in advance. If the situation is emotionally comprehensible to students, it will be because it echoes, touches upon some sympathetic chord in their own histories, reflections, fantasies, hopes and fears. Often we ask questions to which the answers are best left confidential: 'Jot down some of the feelings you think you might have in such a situation . . . See if you can draw a picture or a diagram of how you felt last time somebody behaved like that towards you. . . '. It is a mistake to demand that intimate and intense areas of concern are all shared publicly, even in a small group. Although, as George Eliot observed, silence does not always brood over a full nest, a quiet class is not necessarily a disengaged one. Poetry plays a valuable part in the education of feeling – giving young people a vocabulary with which to explore and discuss things which deeply concern them and which may be aired nowhere else. For this reason a variety of teaching contexts – individual, small group and plenary discussion – is particularly appropriate. If we want to help students own and articulate their perceptions of the world, we must encourage them to talk about what most concerns them but we must also respect their right to some privacy.

What we do not advocate mapping in advance is 'the verbal territory' of a poem. To present a class with a list of hard words that they are about to encounter (probably used in exacting ways) and to drill them in definitions before they are aware of the context, or have any particular desire to acquire such arcane knowledge, seems guaranteed to kill any kind of spontaneous engagement with language, let alone with the situation the poem explores. Eliot observes in his essay on Dante that 'It is a test . . . that genuine poetry can communicate before it is understood'. To see a poem as a verbal hurdle for which a bit of linguistic (or worse still, lit.crit.) limbering-up is the necessary preliminary, is to see poetry merely as an object, an end in itself, rather than an expressive means to an end.

Preliminaries: reading aloud

What Hopkins said about his own verse is true of most of the poetry in this volume: '. . . you must not slovenly read it with the eyes but with your ears, as if the paper were declaiming it at you'. Most poetry is written to be heard; it comes to life in performance. There was no obvious way of producing the *Workshop* so that it was physically impossible to turn to the Thinking/Talking Points before the poem had been read aloud (and then read and reread!) but we would urge that, wherever possible, the poems are read to the class, more than once, even *before* the students look at the poems as marks on a page. Once the text becomes the focus of discussion, it is essential to pause now and again to allow the students to read the poem to themselves at their own pace and from time to time for them again to hear the whole poem read aloud. If you can persuade them to close their eyes while you do that, the benefits will be considerable.

The glossaries

If the most important thing an English teacher does in the classroom is to read aloud, lifting words off the page, we feel the textbook's most important function is to make the surface of the language accessible.

It is odd that although few editions of Shakespeare lack extensive glossaries, prose and poetry equally remote from the language experience of most of our students is usually presented to them bald and intractable. In our experience, a large part of the anxiety/hostility which poetry sometimes produces in readers is no more than confusion and irritation: somebody is playing a game and refusing to divulge the rules. How does any of us feel, confronted by a page of unfamiliar words? Poetry often seems to turn up wrapped in a code – alien, glass-cased – and gets rejected, like the boy in the playground who refuses to talk in a language anybody can understand. And we are surely not the only teachers guilty of lapsing into the game, 'I know the meaning of a long word you don't know . . .' and believing that that was teaching literature? If poetry is misused in this way, to keep students in their place, it is little wonder that it sometimes engenders frustration.

The glossary is a way of giving poetry away, and of making the business of looking it up (part of enjoying most poetry) as effortless and as speedy as possible. It is so boring for everyone in the group to have to trudge through every word that anyone doesn't know! And the small dictionaries usually available to students are little help when it comes to the precise shades of meaning exploited in a poem.

Of course, glossing is a notoriously perilous business. Wishing to 'give poetry away' is easier than doing it. We have tried to be consistent, attempting always to gloss an unfamiliar with a more familiar word or phrase, even at the cost of exactness. Thus the glossed definitions are sometimes no more than starting-points for close verbal scrutiny where you may feel that is appropriate for a particular group. Our concern has been to lead students to the bare prose sense of passages, to help them with their preliminary reading, to guide them into the situation of the poem as quickly as possible. Although poets do sometimes erect barriers to delay explorers, we believe that most would be sorry if students found them characteristically unintelligible.

Like the rest of the text of the *Workshop*, the glossaries have been in a more or less continuous process of revision and simplification for many months and we do not pretend that they could not still be much improved. We should be grateful to receive your comments both on the general principle of glossing and on particular examples which you feel are simply wrong or could be better done.

The Thinking/Talking Points

These are intended to be just that – sometimes to encourage a student's private mulling over of a poem's impact on her/him, sometimes to prompt large or small group discussion. They are not intended and will not work as comprehension exercises. If we have asked a large number of questions it is not in some factitious quest for final answers.

Yet many of the poems we have chosen for this volume use language in a masterly way; part of the enjoyment of them is relishing the peculiar aptness of this phrase, the deliberate ambiguity of that one. To skim a great poem, to read it merely as a bit of clumsily executed prose, a passing illustration of some general theme, is to miss its particular, exciting, exacting richness; there are certain matters of syntax and basic prose sense which we feel need identifying. But on the whole few of our questions will yield answers to be marked right or wrong. Most of them are designed to signpost, to provoke, not to predetermine responses. The good questions will breed further questions from the students.

Working with a whole class, we find it's usually best to give the students some time to do their own thinking and jotting around the Thinking/Talking Points before bringing everyone together to talk. Where feelings, judgements and values are being examined, we shouldn't demand answers to pop out like solutions to maths problems. Forcing the pace is the most common shortcoming in student-teachers working on verse. It is a handy corrective, from time to time, to study one's own processes in coming to terms with the demanding and unfamiliar – perhaps one of Browning's extended pieces – to remind oneself what the experience of meeting an unfamiliar poem is like. The last thing one wants, five minutes after being given a strange text, is to have all sorts of complicated questions fired at one: 'Can you think of seven different meanings for "etiolated" in line 42?' The vague questions are worse than the specific ones: 'Do you like the poem?' If a poem is worth doing, we have to allow it time to unfold itself.

Our job as teachers is to respond to our students' responses; to listen to the stage they have reached and to take care neither to underestimate what the circuits can cope with nor to overload them. Nor to impose an 'adult' reading over one more congruent to the student's own experience of things. It is difficult to strike the proper balance between a pedantic, prescriptive 'reading' of a text and one which is impressionistic, superficial, perhaps foolish. A poem is a meeting-place, a developing dialogue, a collaboration between poetic suggestion and imaginative response. Unlike chapters in textbooks, poems continuously grow with their readers. None of us reads the same *Macbeth* at sixteen and at sixty. We know when a poem is a great one when it means a bit more rather than a bit less each time we read it.

We believe most of our questions, therefore, unlike comprehension questions, are bound to receive different, provisional answers from different students at different stages in their life and language awareness, emotional and intellectual development. It is unnecessary to force the pace. The poem will still be there in a year's time when the student has developed, both as a person and as a reader. The teacher will have grown too. It's very easy, especially when a poem is a particular favourite, to fall into the trap of trying to 'exhaust' it in a couple of lessons which quickly degenerate from collective exploration into one-person expositions: 'What the poet is saying here is . . .'. All that we are likely to exhaust by doing that is our students! When all is said and done, poems are their own best advocates. Once the territory has been opened up, they go on working long after the lesson has been forgotten.

Such teaching requires considerable disinterestedness. It is such a long way from what too many of us experienced in the sixth form or at college where 'Guess the answer in my head' or 'Look it up in *A Reader's Guide*' was too often the name of the lit.crit. game. A poem does not exist independently of a reader: its meaning is a collaboration of text and personal response.

The Assignments

This volume is intended to act as a transitional volume for that most varied, exciting, maddening of school populations, the Third Year. Whilst we certainly believe that the best critical work at any stage is rooted in an imaginative, personal, creative response, there are some assignments here which are intended to develop some of the more impersonal ways of thinking which are fostered in English Literature GCSE syllabuses. The distinction is a matter of balance rather than of kind, between what are primarily imaginative, personal, often oblique or exploratory creative responses to poems and those in which attention to the text of the poem is central. Usually we offer a range of assignments from which the teacher/student may choose. In practice, these distinctions may sometimes be blurred and you may want to adjust an assignment slightly to bring more of a particular text into the spotlight.

We have not attempted to differentiate tasks in some putative order of difficulty. English is one of the few subjects where it is possible to frame a question (e.g. Why did Macbeth kill Duncan?) to which there is a genuinely full spectrum of answers. Designing a dust-jacket or writing a diary entry can certainly involve as high a level of critical interrogation as producing a traditional essay – and be much more interesting to read!

A note on 'assinence and illiteration'

There can be few more depressing experiences than reading A-level unseens which begin: 'The poem has a rhyme scheme ababbadaea' [it doesn't] 'and is written in writhing cutlets in antiseptic metre . . . In line 6 is some illiteration and two words which use assinence: "brown" and "egg-box". The poet uses the image of the girl as a cymbal of suffering . . .' [he doesn't].

Technical terms may have their uses with some academic classes with certain very experienced teachers, but we believe that the dangers of using them far outweigh their utility. For too many students, tracking down a bit of technique becomes not merely a distraction from the theme of the poem but an end in itself; not just an escape from but a block to responding, to seeing the poem at all. And like so many rules ('We were told always to use an apostrophe with an "s" . . .'), technical terminology is frequently misunderstood and misused – by students and, sometimes, even by teachers! Even as an aesthetic tool, we believe jargon is a poor substitute for the student's own language: 'I like the brutal sounds of the harsh words "bent-double . . . beggars under sacks . . . cursing like hags . . ." piled on top of one another. They help you to feel the disgust, the squalor, the ugliness of it all . . .'.

Intellectualising, something which many English graduates have been forced to do to show that an English degree is as real as one in Physics, is something teachers must unlearn quickly if they are to take poetry into the classroom. Sharing a poem means, above all, exploring an intense human experience, with all the uncertainties and dangerous potential which life has. It does call for openness, for a genuine provisionality, a degree of surrender on the part of the teacher: there are no safe, right answers; there will be some challenges which it will not be easy to dismiss. When we feel vulnerable, we fall back on intellectual gymnastics and exclusive terminology. We hope those who have felt uncomfortable talking about poetry as human experience will find that the *Workshop* gives them a structure with which to develop techniques and gain confidence. Once poetry starts to spark in the classroom, nothing can be more exciting.

Lynn and Jeffrey Wood

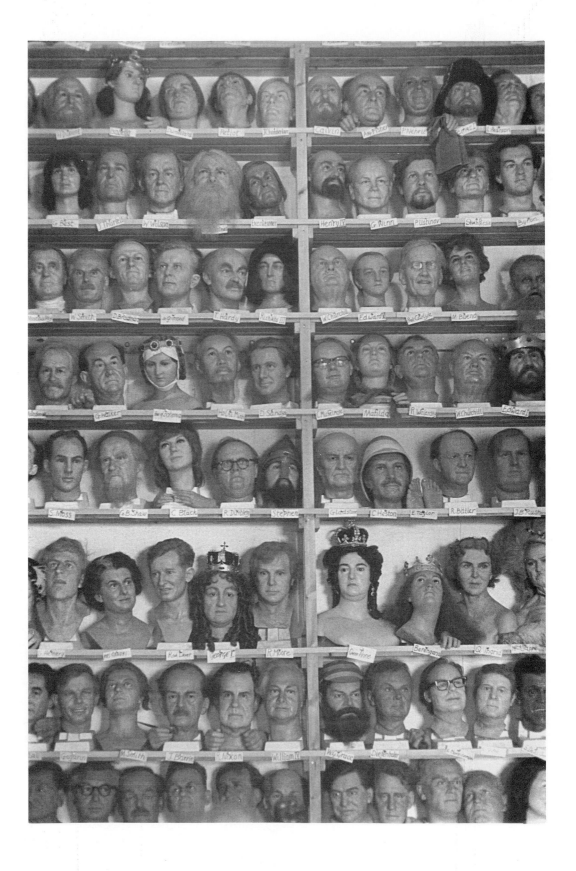

Holub
A BOY'S HEAD

What exactly have you got between your ears?
What do you think a guided tour of your brain would reveal?

Assignment 1

o   Draw a not-too-serious labelled diagram of your thinking-apparatus, showing the various bits that make it like nobody else's.

Here is Miroslav Holub's version.

A Boy's Head

In it there is a space-ship
and a project
for doing away with piano lessons.

And there is
Noah's ark,   5
which shall be first.

And there is
an entirely new bird,
an entirely new hare,
an entirely new bumble-bee.   10

There is a river
that flows upwards.

There is a multiplication table.

There is anti-matter.

And it just cannot be trimmed.   15

I believe
that only what cannot be trimmed
is a head.

There is much promise
in the circumstance   20
that so many people have heads.

☆

Thinking/Talking Points

▷ Where do you think the boy is? Have you any idea how old he might be?

▷ What do you think this means:
'And there is
an entirely new bird,
an entirely new hare,
an entirely new bumble-bee.'

▷ How might a river flow upwards?
See if you can suggest what anti-matter is.

▷ What do you think the poet means when he says
'. . . only what cannot be trimmed
is a head'?

▷ Try explaining the final verse in your own words.

Now read through the poem again a couple of times before you tackle the second assignment.

Assignment 2

○ Write your own version of Holub's poem – about your own head or about that of somebody you know well.

★

8

MIRROR

Does your toothbrush grin at you each morning?
Have you ever caught the kitchen clock winking at the washing-machine?

Do you sometimes imagine that lifeless things such as teapots, tables and
televisions have personalities?
What sort of character do you think a comfortable armchair might be? Or a
blue plastic lampshade?

How do you think a doormat feels about being walked over by everyone?
What tales about your family could your telephone tell?
Have you ever wondered what the mirror sees in you?

Read through this poem a few times before considering the points which
follow.

Mirror

I am silver and exact. I have no preconceptions.
Whatever I see I swallow immediately
Just as it is, unmisted by love or dislike.
I am not cruel, only truthful –
The eye of a little god, four-cornered.   5
Most of the time I meditate on the opposite wall.
It is pink, with speckles. I have looked at it so long
I think it is a part of my heart. But it flickers.
Faces and darkness separate us over and over.

Now I am a lake. A woman bends over me,   10
Searching my reaches for what she really is.
Then she turns to those liars, the candles or the moon.
I see her back, and reflect it faithfully.
She rewards me with tears and an agitation of hands.
I am important to her. She comes and goes.   15
Each morning it is her face that replaces the darkness.
In me she has drowned a young girl, and in me an old woman
Rises toward her day after day, like a terrible fish.

I have no preconceptions
I am impartial, I don't
make up my mind about
things until I see them.
unmisted *unclouded.*

meditate on *think about.*

reaches *depths.*

agitation of hands *restless*
wringing of hands.

☆

Thinking/Talking Points

▷ Suggest half-a-dozen words of your own to describe this mirror's personality. Which of the poet's words give you that impression?

▷ What do you think the woman is hoping to see in the mirror? What does she find?

▷ Why do you think the mirror calls candles and the moon 'liars'?

▷ See if you can rewrite the last two lines of the poem in your own words.

▷ Do you think being completely truthful is always right? Can a mirror be terrifying?

Read through the poem again a few times to see what else deserves attention. Are there any words or phrases you don't understand, any interesting details you hadn't noticed?

Assignments

○ Write a similar piece of your own in which a mirror looks closely at somebody (perhaps someone you know well).

○ Describe as fully as you can what you see when you look in the mirror.

○ Write your own piece in which some apparently lifeless object in your house 'tells all' about the people who take it for granted (e.g. the fridge; the telephone; a lamp; the television; the computer; a carpet; the sofa; the front door; the garden shed; the car).
Try to give your object a way of talking which suits its personality. You may write in verse or in prose.

★

Brooke
from THE GREAT LOVER

What could a detective tell about you, just from looking through the contents of your pockets or your schoolbag? Or by inspecting your bedroom?

Do your belongings tell others much about you? (e.g. Do you like to wear particular colours? Have you got any keepsakes? Do you gnaw pens, decorate your bicycle, tie your shoes in a special way? Is your hairstyle *you*? Or your pencil-case or your collections?)
Which of all your things would it hurt you most to lose?

Which everyday experiences do you like most/least (e.g. combing your hair; having breakfast; travelling to school; getting home)?
What's your favourite weather?

Imagine, in a hundred years' time, your great-granddaughter or grandson coming across a trunkful of your things. What might she or he find?

If in fifty years' time your grandchild met an old schoolfriend of yours, what habits, tastes, oddities might he/she hear about?

Read through this extract from Brooke's poem, *The Great Lover*, a few times before thinking about the points which follow.

from The Great Lover

These I have loved:
  White plates and cups, clean-gleaming,
Ringed with blue lines; and feathery, faery dust;
Wet roofs, beneath the lamp-light; the strong crust
Of friendly bread; and many-tasting food;   5
Rainbows; and the blue bitter smoke of wood;
And radiant raindrops couching in cool flowers;   **radiant** *bright, glistening.*
And flowers themselves, that sway through sunny hours,   **couching** *resting, nestling.*
Dreaming of moths that drink them under the moon;
Then, the cool kindliness of sheets, that soon   10
Smooth away trouble; and the rough male kiss
Of blankets; grainy wood; live hair that is
Shining and free; blue-massing clouds; the keen   **keen, unpassioned** *hard,*
Unpassioned beauty of a great machine;   *without emotion, austere,*
unfeeling.
The benison of hot water; furs to touch;   15   **benison** *blessing.*
The good smell of old clothes; and other such –
The comfortable smell of friendly fingers,
Hair's fragrance, and the musty reek that lingers   **musty reek** *mouldy, stale*
About dead leaves and last year's ferns . . .   *smell.*

12

Dear names,   20
And thousand others throng to me! Royal flames;   *throng* come in crowds.
Sweet water's dimpling laugh from tap or spring;
Holes in the ground; and voices that do sing:
Voices in laughter, too; and body's pain,
Soon turned to peace; and the deep-panting train;   25
Firm sands; the little dulling edge of foam
That browns and dwindles as the wave goes home;   *dwindles* gets smaller.
And washen stones, gay for an hour; the cold
Graveness of iron; moist black earthen mould;   *graveness* heaviness,
Sleep; and high places; footprints in the dew;   30   *seriousness.*
And oaks; and brown horse-chestnuts, glossy-new; —   *earthen mould* compost,
And new-peeled sticks; and shining pools on grass; —   *humus.*
All these have been my loves.

Thinking/Talking Points

▷   See if you can find examples of each of these:
          things the speaker loves to see
          things he loves to listen to
          things he loves to touch
          things he loves to taste
          things he loves to smell
          things he finds it lovely to think about
          things he loves to experience

▷   What overall impression of the speaker's personality do all these details give
     you? Jot down a few words to describe him.

     Read through the poem again a couple of times and then choose your
     assignment.

Assignments

○   Write your own version of Brooke's poem.
     You might begin by listing two or three of each of the things you love to hear,
     taste, smell, touch and look at.
     Then think of the places, people, occasions, tasks, amusements, weather that
     you love.
     Try to collect together both the big and little things which mean most to you.
     Try to be as precise as possible to help the reader share your particular pleasure.
     (e.g. If you love fireworks, is it the hiss and clatter, the sulphur smell, the
     swirling patterns which they make in the black sky, that you love?)

○   *Grandmother's/Grandfather's Trunk*
Set the scene: today's date plus seventy years.
Write as if you are your grandchild who has heard so much about you but never seen even a photograph of you. Explain why.
One day, she/he has to clear the attic of your old house and comes across the dusty trunk.
What does it contain? (Photographs? Souvenirs? Old school reports? Love letters? Old tickets and newspaper cuttings? A diary? A list of new year's resolutions for 1999?)
What impression of *you* slowly emerges?
How does your grandchild feel about her/his unknown ancestor?

○   Make a collage picture either to illustrate the poem or to give the viewer an idea of yourself.

Further reading

Keith Waterhouse   *There is a Happy Land*

★

= *Abse* =
ODD

Where do you feel most relaxed? At home? At someone else's house? At a party? At school? Out with your friends? Alone?

Think of the place you most enjoy visiting. Why do you like it?
Are there particular buildings, trees, signs which are its 'landmarks'?

Where do you most dislike being?
What exactly is it about that place which annoys/worries/depresses you?

How would you describe the personality of the area where you live (e.g. cosy; snooty; scruffy; friendly; tight-lipped; jolly; sombre)?
What are the 'landmarks' of your neighbourhood (e.g. Mrs Jones's garden full of gnomes; the comfy corner shop; the lads at the corner)?

Read this poem a couple of times and then consider the points which follow.

Odd

In front of our house in Golders Green
the lawn, like a cliché, mutters 'Rose bushes'.
The whole suburb is very respectable.
Ugly men drive past in funeral suits,
from their necks you can tell they're overweight.   5

Sodium lamp-posts, at night, hose empty roads
with gold which treacles over pavement trees,
polishes brittle hedges, clings on closed, parked cars.
If a light should fly on in an upstairs room
odds on two someones are going to sleep.   10

It's unusual to meet a beggar,
you hardly ever see a someone drunk.
It's a nice, clean, quiet, religious place.
For my part, now and then, I want to scream:
thus, by the neighbours, am considered odd.   15

From the sensible wastes of Golders Green
I journey to Soho where a job owns me.
Soho is not a respectable place.
Underweight women in the gamiest of skirts
bleed a smile of false teeth at ugly men.   20

cliché something once original and striking but now common.
suburb a residential area on the fringe of a big city.

treacles pours like treacle.

wastes dull, empty, lifeless places.

gamiest very provocative, sexy.

15

Later, the dark is shabby with paste electric
of peeporamas, brothels, clubs and pubs,
restaurants that sport sallow waiters who cough.
If a light should fly on in an upstairs room
odds on two someones are going to bed.   25

It's customary to see many beggars,
common to meet people roaring and drunk.
It's a nice, loud, dirty, irreligious place.
For my part, now and then, I want to scream:
thus, by Soho friends, am considered odd.   30

paste electric neon-lit
advertisements.

sallow a sickly yellow
colour.

customary usual.

☆

Thinking/Talking Points

▷ Do you know what we usually mean by a cliché?
Can you think of an example?
What do you think the speaker means when he says his lawn is like a cliché?
What other 'clichés' do you imagine in the streets of Golders Green?

▷ Describe in your own words the effects which the lighting of the street lamps
has.

▷ Sum up the character of Golders Green in your own words.
Describe a couple of people you might see walking along the road.
Why do you think the fact that the place is
'nice, clean, quiet, religious'
makes the speaker want to scream?

▷ Look again at stanza 4.
What do you think these phrases mean:
'a job *owns* me', '*bleed* a smile of false teeth'?

▷ What makes night time in Soho so different from night time in Golders Green?

▷ 'It's a nice, loud, dirty, irreligious place.'
Does 'nice' mean the same here as in line 13?
Do you think the speaker prefers Soho to Golders Green?
Why do you think Soho, too, sometimes makes him want to scream?

Read through the poem again before selecting an assignment.

Assignments

○ Make a picture, with the poet at the centre, suggesting the two worlds he
inhabits.

○ *Two Pictures of Me*
Write about your behaviour and your feelings in two very different places or
situations (e.g. yourself at home and yourself at school; yourself in a religious
place and yourself at a party; yourself with your parents and yourself with
friends; yourself alone and yourself in company).

★

CHILDREN

Do you think your parents really *know* you?
If they were asked by a neighbour or a teacher to describe you, what are some of the things they might say?
If somebody asked your parents what they hoped you'd be doing in ten years' time, what do you think they would suggest?
Are your hopes for your future the same as theirs?
What do you think must be the most difficult thing about being a parent?

Children

Whether by careless accident
or careful plan
we are where they begin.

They grow in us
like germs or fictions   5   *fictions* stories, fantasies.
and we grow big with them.

Red, mewling strangers   *mewling* crying.
they tear our thresholds   *threshold* the point of exit,
and immediately we love them.   birth channel.

When people say   10
they look like us
we smile and blush.

We listen for their cries
as if we felt their pain
and hunger deep in us   15

and hold them tightly
in our arms as if we'd found
a lost part of ourselves.

We want to give them
all the things we never had,   20
to make it up to them

for all the times
when we were hurt or sad,
to start again and put right
                                                             run in front of them with
our mistakes in them,   25   *warning flags* as people
to run in front of them   *used to run in front of the*
with warning flags.   *first motor cars to warn*
                                                             pedestrians.

We who've failed to be
the authors of our lives
write theirs.   *30*

We make them heroes,
stars whose happy endings
will scatter light in ours.

We feed them with our dreams
then wait and watch   *35*
like gardeners for flowers.

☆

Thinking/Talking Points

▷ What positive things is this poem saying about the ways parents look after and
   feel about their children?

▷ Which statements in the poem could be seen as criticisms of the ways some
   parents regard and treat their children?

Assignments

○ Write a poem in a similar style called *Parents*, in which you try to show how
   children see and feel about those very important people.

○ *Letter to Parents*
   You have been asked to contribute to *Parents' Magazine*.
   Your article, based partly upon your own experiences and/or those of your
   friends, is intended to be *either* a serious *or* a humorous piece in which you
   describe/discuss some of the common mistakes parents make in bringing up
   their children, particularly when they reach the age of fourteen.
   Give your readers some advice about what makes a 'good parent'.

○ *Happy Families*
   Write a story in which there is a conflict between somebody of your own age
   and his/her parents about what they see as good for him/her.

Some further reading

Short stories:
John Wain   *Manhood*
Doris Lessing   *Through the Tunnel*

Autobiography:
Roald Dahl   *Boy*
Bob Geldof   *Is That It?*

★

A POISON TREE

What do you think Anger looks like? (e.g. A spluttering volcano? A savage bird? A howling wind? Purple zigzags?)

Assignment

○ See if you can draw a picture of Anger.

What things make you angry?

Think of a time when you were furious with someone.
What did being angry feel like?
What did you want to do?

Have you ever been angry with someone for days?
What finally happened to the anger?

When you're angry with somebody, do you think it's better to tell them or to keep your feelings to yourself?

Is it easier to show anger to people you do like or people you don't like?
What happens to your anger when you hide it?
Do you ever *enjoy* being angry?

Read through this poem a few times before thinking about the points which follow.

A Poison Tree

I was angry with my friend:
I told my wrath, my wrath did end.   **wrath** *anger, fury.*
I was angry with my foe: **foe** *enemy.*
I told it not, my wrath did grow.

And I water'd it in fears,   5
Night and morning with my tears;
And I sunned it with smiles,
And with soft deceitful wiles.   **wiles** *tricks, tactics.*

And it grew both day and night,
Till it bore an apple bright;   10
And my foe beheld it shine,
And he knew that it was mine,

And into my garden stole
When the night had veil'd the pole:
In the morning glad I see   15
My foe outstretch'd beneath the tree.

stole crept.

pole the sky, the heavens.

Thinking/Talking Points

▷ Why was the speaker's anger with his friend soon over?

▷ See if you can describe in your own words what happened to the anger the speaker felt for his enemy. (Look particularly at stanza 2.)

▷ At the end of the poem, the speaker says that he feels *glad*.
Suggest some other words or phrases to describe the way he may have been feeling.

▷ Can you explain why the poem is called *A Poison Tree*?

Read through the poem again a few times and then choose your assignment.

Assignments

○ Draw a cartoon strip or a picture to illustrate Blake's poem.

○ *A Poison Tree*
Write a story of your own about an incident (true or imaginary) in which you nurse your anger until something terrible happens.

○ In a similar style, write a poem about one of these feelings: fear; envy; jealousy; greed; ambition; hatred.
See if you can find a picture like Blake's apple to stand for the feeling.
You may like to illustrate your work.

○ *I Told It Not*
Write about a time when having to keep your feelings to yourself made you angry/frustrated/unhappy/cruel/lonely or confused.

Further reading

John Wain   *A Message from the Pig Man*

SONG OF THE WAGONDRIVER

McColl
THE FIREMAN'S NOT FOR ME

Song of the Wagondriver

My first love was the ten-ton truck
They gave me when I started,
And though she played the bitch with me
I grieved when we were parted.

Since then I've had a dozen more,   5
The wound was quick to heal,
And now it's easier to say
I'm married to my wheel.

I've trunked it north, I've trunked it south,
On wagons good and bad,   10
But none was ever really like
The first I ever had.

trunked it followed the main roads (motorways).

The life is hard, the hours are long,
Sometimes I cease to feel,
But I go on, for it seems to me   15
I'm married to my wheel.

Often I think of my home and kids,
Out on the road at night,
And think of taking a local job
Provided the money's right.   20

Two nights a week I see my wife,
And eat a decent meal,
But otherwise, for all my life,
I'm married to my wheel.

The Fireman's Not for Me

Come all you young maidens, take warning from me,
  Shun all engine firemen and their company;
He'll tell you he loves you and all kinds of lies,
  But the one that he loves is the train that he drives.

shun avoid, keep away from.

21

I once loved a fireman and he said he loved me;　　　　　5
　　He took me a-walking into the country;
He hugged me and kissed me and gazed in my eyes,
　　And said, 'You're as nice as the eight-fortyfive!'

He said, 'My dear Molly, just say you'll be mine;
　　Just give me the signal and let's clear the line.　　　10
My fires they are burning and the steam it is high —
　　If you don't take the brakes off I think I will die.'

I gave him my answer, saying, 'Don't make so free!'
　　For no loco fireman shall ever have me!
He'll take all your love and then, when you're in need,　　15
　　He races away at the top of his speed.

A sailor comes home when his voyage is done,
　　A soldier gets weary of following the drum,
A collier will cleave to his loved one for life —
　　But a fireman's one love is the engine, his wife!　　　20

Thinking/Talking Points

▷　What would you like to do when you leave school?
　　Jot down some of the things which you will look for in a job.

▷　What do you think people mean when they say somebody is 'married to
　　her/his work'?

▷　Which do you think is more important: work or family life?

▷　Why do you think the speakers feel as they do?
　　With which of them do you have more sympathy? Why?

Assignment

○　Write your own song.
　　Write *either* from the point of view of the working husband/wife *or* from the
　　point of view of the wife/husband left at home.
　　Suggested titles:　　*Travelling Salesman's Wife's Lament*
　　　　　　　　　　　　Song of the Astronaut
　　　　　　　　　　　　Ballad of the Prime Minister's Husband
　　　　　　　　　　　　The Butcher's Carol
　　　　　　　　　　　　Chant of a Footballer's Girl
　　You may like to write the song to fit a well-known tune.

★

A CONSTABLE CALLS

As you are walking home tonight, you see a police car pulled up outside your house. How do you feel?

What makes a police officer's visit different from anyone else's (from a vicar's, for example, or a doctor's)?

Is there anything about a police officer's uniform or behaviour which makes it difficult for you to remember that he/she is just someone doing a job?

Read through this poem a couple of times and then think about the points which follow.

A Constable Calls

His bicycle stood at the window-sill,
The rubber cowl of a mud-splasher   **cowl** *hood.*
Skirting the front mudguard,
Its fat black handlegrips

Heating in the sunlight, the 'spud'   5
Of the dynamo gleaming and cocked back,
The pedal treads hanging relieved
Of the boot of the law.

His cap was upside down
On the floor, next his chair,   10
The line of its pressure ran like a bevel   **bevel** *groove made by a*
In his slightly sweating hair.   *triangular tool.*

He had unstrapped
The heavy ledger, and my father   **ledger** *book in which facts*
Was making tillage returns   15   *and figures are recorded.*
In acres, roods, and perches.   **tillage returns** *records of*
                                              what crops a farmer has
                                              planted.
                                              acres, roods, perches
Arithmetic and fear   *measures of land.*
I sat staring at the polished holster
With its buttoned flap, the braid cord   **braid cord** *strong string*
Looped into the revolver butt.   20   *made of strands twisted*
                                              together.
                                              butt *handle.*

'Any other root crops?
Mangolds? Marrowstems? Anything like that?'   **mangolds** *large coarse beet,*
'No.' But was there not a line   *cattle food.*
Of turnips where the seed ran out   **marrowstems** *a type of*
                                              kale that is grown for
                                              animal fodder.
In the potato field? I assumed   25
Small guilts and sat
Imagining the black hole in the barracks.   **baton-case** *leather case*
He stood up, shifted the baton-case   *holding the policeman's*
                                              truncheon.

23

Further round on his belt,
Closed the domesday book,   30   **domesday book** *like the*
Fitted his cap back with two hands,   *Domesday Book of 1086 in*
And looked at me as he said goodbye.   *which all landholdings in*
                                                                   England were very precisely
                                                                   registered.
A shadow bobbed in the window.
He was snapping the carrier spring
Over the ledger. His boot pushed off   35
And the bicycle ticked, ticked, ticked.

☆

Thinking/Talking Points

▷   What did the poem's title lead you to expect?

▷   What do the details describing the policeman's bicycle suggest about the
    personality of its rider?

▷   Look again at stanza 3.
    Do the details we are given there change the way we see the constable?

▷   Look again at stanza 4.
    Can you explain what is going on?

▷   What thoughts and feelings are passing through the speaker's mind as her/his
    father and the policeman talk?
    Why do you think the child's attention is fixed on the holster?

▷   Why does the speaker have to assume 'small guilts'? (line 26)
    What do you think 'the black hole' he/she imagines is?

▷   What expression do you imagine on the policeman's face when he looks at the
    child and says goodbye?
    How do you think the child is feeling?

▷   Do you like the way the poem ends? Why? Why not?

    Read through the poem again to see what else deserves attention before
    choosing your assignment.

Assignments

○   Imagine you are the policeman, cycling away.
    Record your feelings and suspicions.
    Are you satisfied with the entry you have made in your 'domesday book'?

○   *A Constable Calls*
    Imagine a visit to your house by a police officer on a routine matter (e.g. the
    dog's been annoying a neighbour).
    As she/he is about to leave, you are asked a simple question about one of your
    friends.
    Write a story about the incident.
    See if you can make the reader feel the tension between what you know and
    what you say.
    You may write your piece either as a poem or as a short story.

24   ★

THE BURGLARY

Imagine a burglar. Describe him/her.

Do you think burglars feel anything about the people they steal from?
Can you imagine a burglar taking pride in his/her work?

You are writing a story about a 'job' as if the burglar is telling it.
What descriptive details do you think would help to make your story feel
'authentic', convincing?

When you have thought about how you might write about a burglary, read
through this poem a couple of times. Then consider the points which follow.

The Burglary

It's two o'clock now; somebody's pausing in the street
to turn up his collar. The night's black: distraught
with chimney-toppling wind and harsh rain –
see, the wet's soaking in on the end-gable,
and the frothing torrent, overspilling the broken drain,   5

accosts the pavement with incoherent babble.
There is the house we want: how easy to burgle,
with its dark trees, and the lawn set back from the road;
the owners will be in bed now – the old couple;
you've got the position of the safe? – Yes, I know the code.   10

The cock's going mad up there on the church steeple;
the wind's enormous – will it ever stifle;
still, its noise, and the rain's are with us, I daresay,
they'll cover what we make, if we go careful
round by the greenhouse, and in at the back way.   15

Here's the broken sash I mentioned; – no need to be fearful,
watch how I do it: these fingers are facile
with the practice I've had on worse nights than this.
I tell you, the whole thing's going to be a doddle:
the way I've got it worked out, we can't miss.   20

Although, God knows, most things turn out a muddle,
and it only confuses more to look for a moral.
Wherever I've been the wind and rain's blown; –
I've done my best to hang on, as they tried to whittle
the name from the action, the flesh away from the bone,   25

distraught *agitated, upset.*

end-gable *triangular wall holding up the sloping sides of a roof.*
torrent *heavy downpour of rain.*
accosts . . . with incoherent babble *it's as if the water is chattering wildly, asking for something, in a language the pavement doesn't understand.*
cock *weather vane.*
stifle *subside.*

sash *a window which opens vertically.*
facile *quick, skilful.*

a doddle *easy.*

moral *an explanation of why things happen as they do.*
whittle *scrape away.*

but I think, sometimes, I'm fighting a losing battle.
So many bad nights; so many strange homes to burgle;
and every job done with a mate I don't know: —
oh, you're all right; I don't mean to be personal,
but when the day breaks, you'll have your orders, and go.   *30*

Then, the next time the foul weather howls in the ginnel;   **ginnel** *alleyway.*
when the slates slide, the brimming gutters gurgle;   **brimming** *about to*
there'll be another lad I've never seen before,   *overflow.*
with the rest of the knowledge that makes the job possible
as I ease up a window or skeleton-key a door.   *35*   **skeleton-key** *use an illegal*
                                                                          master-key.

Still, it's my only life, and I've no quarrel
with the boss's methods; — apart from the odd quibble   **quibble** *unimportant*
about allowances and fair rates of pay,   *disagreement.*
or the difficult routes I often have to travel,
or the fact that I never get a holiday.   *40*

Most of the time, though, I'm glad of mere survival,
even at the stormiest hour of the darkest vigil.   **vigil** *keeping watch.*
. . . Here's the hall door; under the stairs, you said?
This one's easy, because the old folk are feeble,
and lie in their curtained room, sleeping like the dead.   *45*

Sometimes, believe me, it's a lot more trouble,
when you've got to be silent, and move as though through
                                                         treacle.
Now hold your breath while I let these tumblers click . . .   **tumblers** *locking*
I've done these many a time . . . a well known model;   *mechanism.*
one more turn now . . . Yes; that does the trick.   *50*

Nothing inside? The same recurrent muddle;   **recurrent** *repeated.*
I think the most careful plan's a bloody marvel
if it plays you true, if nothing at all goes wrong.
Well, let's be off; we've another place to tackle
under the blown, black, rain; and the dawn won't be long   *55*

when the wind will drop, and the rain become a drizzle,
and you'll go your way. Leaving me the bedraggled   **bedraggled** *wet and*
remnants of night, that walk within the head   *scruffy.*
long after the sun-shot gutters cease to trickle,
and I draw my curtains, and topple into bed.   *60*

☆

Thinking/Talking Points

▷ Which details help set the scene?

▷ Why do you think the poet chose to write in the present tense?
   What's the effect of his 'chatty' style?

▷ How do you picture 'the old couple'?
   Does the way you imagine them affect how you feel about the burglar?

▷ Is this burglar a man or a woman? What's the evidence?

▷ How does the burglar feel about his/her trade?
   Which details give you that impression?

▷ What's your impression of the boss?

▷ How would you describe the burglar's mood at the end?
   What do you feel about him/her?

   Read through the poem again a couple of times before planning your
   assignment.

Assignment

○ Use the poem as a model and write your own piece, in verse or prose, about
   one of the following 'jobs' seen through the eyes of the main character:
      a shoplifting expedition
      a bouncer working at a shady nightclub
      a debt-collector on his rounds
      someone breaking into school
      the planting of a terrorist bomb
   Include plenty of scene-setting detail.
   Try to bring out the story-teller's mixed feelings about the job he/she finds
   himself doing.
   Use a style of talking which suits the character.
   Don't include too much action: concentrate on the speaker's thoughts and
   feelings.

★

OUR VILLAGE –
BY A VILLAGER

Think of the district where you live. Can you imagine anyone making a film about it or mentioning it in a guidebook?

What's the most interesting feature of your neighbourhood?
Who is the oldest inhabitant?
How would a traveller know when she/he got there?
Where would you go for a chat?
Whose is the scruffiest garden?
Who keeps the oddest pet?
Who is the local flirt/gossip/eccentric?
Where could you find someone to mend your bike or television?
Where do children play in summer? Where do the lads hang out at weekends?
Who's got the loudest laugh/the silliest walk/the wildest clothes?
What's the most interesting piece of graffiti in your neighbourhood?

Our Village – By a Villager

Our village, that's to say not Miss Mitford's village, but our
　　village of Bullock Smithy,
Is come into by an avenue of trees, three oak pollards, two
　　elders, and a withy;
And in the middle, there's a green of about not exceeding an
　　acre and a half;
It's common to all, and fed off by nineteen cows, six ponies,
　　three horses, five asses, two foals, seven pigs, and a calf!
Besides a pond in the middle, as is held by a similar sort of
　　common law lease,
And contains twenty ducks, six drakes, three ganders, two dead
　　dogs, four drowned kittens, and twelve geese.
Of course the green's cropt very close, and does famous for
　　bowling when the little village boys play at cricket;
Only some horse, or pig, or cow, or great jackass, is sure to come
　　and stand right before the wicket.
There's fifty-five private houses, let alone barns and workshops,
　　and pigstyes, and poultry huts, and such-like sheds;
With plenty of public-houses – two Foxes, one Green Man,
　　three Bunch of Grapes, one Crown, and six King's Heads.
The Green Man is reckoned the best, as the only one that for
　　love or money can raise
A postilion, a blue jacket, two deplorable lame white horses,
　　and a ramshackled 'neat postchaise'.

pollards *trees whose branches have been lopped short.*
withy *willow.*

5 **as is held by a similar sort of common law lease** *which is also regarded as public property.*

10 **postilion** *a servant who rides on one of the horses drawing a carriage.* **deplorable** *wretched.* **ramshackled** *rickety.* **postchaise** *horse-drawn carriage.*

There's one parish church for all the people, whatsoever may be
    their ranks in life or their degrees.

ranks . . . or . . . degrees social standing, class.

Except one very damp, small, dark, freezing-cold little
    Methodist chapel of Ease;

chapel of Ease small chapel.

And close by the church-yard there's a stone-mason's yard, that
    when the time is seasonable   15

Will furnish with afflictions sore and marble urns and cherubims
    very low and reasonable.

afflictions sore and marble urns and cherubims carved messages of regret and other graveyard furniture.

There's a cage, comfortable enough, I've been in it with old
    Jack Jeffrey and Tom Pike;

For the Green Man next door will send you in ale, gin, or
    anything else you like.

I can't speak of the stocks, as nothing remains of them but the
    upright post;

stocks a device for punishing offenders which consisted of a timber frame which confined the feet.

But the pound is kept in repairs for the sake of Cob's horse, as is
    always there almost.   20

pound place where stray cattle are kept.

There's a smithy of course, where that queer sort of a chap in
    his way, Old Joe Bradley,

smithy blacksmith's.

Perpetually hammers and stammers, for he stutters and shoes
    horses very badly.

perpetually day in, day out.

There's a shop of all sorts, that sells everything, kept by the
    widow of Mr Task;

But when you go there, it's ten to one she's out of everything
    you ask.

You'll know her house by the swarm of boys, like flies, about
    the old sugary cask: 25

cask barrel.

There are six empty houses, and not so well papered inside as
    out,

For bill-stickers won't beware, but sticks notices of sales and
    election placards all about.

That's the Doctor's with a green door, where the garden pots in
    the windows is seen;

A weakly monthly rose that don't blow, and a dead geranium,
    and a tea-plant with five black leaves and one green.

blow bloom.

As for hollyoaks at the cottage doors, and honeysuckles and
    jasmines, you may go and whistle;   30

hollyoaks hollyhocks.

But the Tailor's front garden grows two cabbages, a dock, a
    ha'porth of pennyroyal, two dandelions, and a thistle.

pennyroyal a kind of mint.

There are three small orchards – Mr Busby's the schoolmaster's
    is the chief –

With two pear-trees that don't bear; one plum and an apple, that
    every year is stripped by a thief.

There's another small day-school too, kept by the respectable
    Mrs Gaby.

A select establishment, for six little boys and one big, and four
    little girls and a baby;   35

There's a rectory, with pointed gables and strange odd chimneys
    that never smokes.

the rector don't live on his living the vicar doesn't live in the parish which pays him.

For the rector don't live on his living like other Christian sort of folks;

29

There's a barber's, once a week well filled with rough black-
    bearded shock-headed churls,   *churls* rough fellows.
And a window with two feminine men's heads, and two
    masculine ladies in false curls;
There's a butcher's, and a carpenter's, and a plumber's, and a
    small greengrocer's and a baker,   40
But he won't bake on Sunday, and there's a sexton that's a   *sexton* gravedigger.
    coal-merchant besides, and an undertaker;
And a toyshop, but not a whole one, for a village can't compare
    with the London shops;
One window sells drums, dolls, kites, carts, bats, Clout's balls,   *Clout's balls* (?) balls made
    and the other sells malt and hops.   *of cloth.*
                                                                     malt and hops ingredients
And Mrs Brown, in domestic economy not to be a bit behind her   *for making beer.*
    betters,   *domestic economy*
Lets her house to a milliner, a watchmaker, a rat-catcher, a   *household management.*
    cobbler, lives in it herself, and it's the post-office for letters. 45 *milliner* hat-maker.
Now I've gone through all the village – aye, from end to end,
    save and except one more house,
But I haven't come to that – and I hope I never shall – and that's   *Poor House* hostel for the
    the Village Poor House!   *very poor.*

Thinking/Talking Points

▷ What is your impression of the speaker and his village?
   When do you think the poem was written? Why?

▷ Why do you think he is so fussy about the sizes and numbers of things in his
   catalogue? What sort of voice do you hear him talking in?

▷ Pick out half-a-dozen details from the poem which would be unlikely to be
   included in a guidebook.

▷ What do you think 'the cage' could be?
   Why do you think the speaker found himself inside it?

▷ Is Old Joe Bradley the sort of blacksmith you'd expect to find in a picture-
   postcard village?

▷ How do you imagine lessons at Mrs Gaby's establishment?

Read through the poem again and then choose your assignment.

Assignments

○ *Our Street/Village/Town/City/Neighbourhood*
   Begin by writing down as many facts as you can about your neighbourhood.
   How would we know when we got there? What sort of houses, shops and
   landmarks might we notice? What characters might we come across? What
   makes the area well-known . . . for better or worse?!
   Then decide which details are worth keeping. Develop and shape them into a
   poem like Hood's.

○ Produce some illustrations for *Our Village*.

★

Before you read this poem, think about what pictures, what stories, the title
The Highwayman suggests to you.

The Highwayman

Part I

The wind was a torrent of darkness among the gusty trees,
The moon was a ghostly galleon tossed upon cloudy seas.
The road was a ribbon of moonlight over the purple moor,
And the highwayman came riding –
    Riding – riding –   5
The highwayman came riding, up to the old inn-door.

galleon *a stately sailing ship.*

He'd a French cocked-hat on his forehead, a bunch of lace at his
                              chin,
A coat of the claret velvet, and breeches of brown doe-skin.
They fitted with never a wrinkle. His boots were up to the thigh.
And he rode with a jewelled twinkle,   10
    His pistol butts a-twinkle,
His rapier hilt a-twinkle, under the jewelled sky.

cocked-hat *three-cornered hat with upturned brim.*
claret *dark red.*
breeches *trousers.*
butt *handle.*
rapier hilt *handle of a long thin sword.*

Over the cobbles he clattered and clashed in the dark inn-yard.
He tapped with his whip on the shutters, but all was locked and
                              barred.
He whistled a tune to the window, and who should be waiting
                         there   15
But the landlord's black-eyed daughter,
    Bess, the landlord's daughter,
Plaiting a dark red love-knot into her long black hair.

And dark in the dark old inn-yard a stable-wicket creaked
Where Tim the ostler listened. His face was white and peaked.   20
His eyes were hollows of madness, his hair like mouldy hay,
But he loved the landlord's daughter,
    The landlord's red-lipped daughter.
Dumb as a dog he listened, and he heard the robber say –

wicket *small gate.*

'One kiss, my bonny sweetheart, I'm after a prize to-night,   25
But I shall be back with the yellow gold before the morning light;
Yet, if they press me sharply, and harry me through the day,
Then look for me by moonlight,
    Watch for me by moonlight,
I'll come to thee by moonlight, though hell should bar the way.'   30

harry *harrass, trouble.*

He rose upright in the stirrups. He scarce could reach her hand,
But she loosened her hair i'the casement. His face burnt like a
                                                                brand
As the black cascade of perfume came tumbling over his breast;
And he kissed its waves in the moonlight,
        (Oh, sweet black waves in the moonlight!)   35
Then he tugged at his rein in the moonlight, and galloped away
                                                        to the west.

casement *window.*
brand *burning piece of wood.*
cascade *like a waterfall.*

Part II

He did not come in the dawning. He did not come at noon;
And out o' the tawny sunset, before the rise o' the moon,
When the road was a gipsy's ribbon, looping the purple moor,
A red-coat troop came marching —   40
        Marching — marching —
King George's men came marching, up to the old inn-door.

tawny *the colour of a lion.*

red-coat *a soldier in scarlet uniform.*

They said no word to the landlord. They drank his ale instead.
But they gagged his daughter, and bound her, to the foot of her
                                                        narrow bed.
Two of them knelt at her casement, with muskets at their side!   45
There was a death at every window;
        And hell at one dark window;
For Bess could see, through her casement, the road that *he* would
                                                        ride.

musket *an early type of rifle.*

They had tied her up to attention, with many a sniggering jest.
They had bound a musket beside her, with the muzzle beneath
                                                        her breast! 50
'Now, keep good watch!' and they kissed her.
        She heard the dead man say —
Look for me by moonlight;
        Watch for me by moonlight;
I'll come to thee by moonlight, though hell should bar the way!   55

muzzle *mouth of a gun.*

She twisted her hands behind her; but all the knots held good!
She writhed her hands till her fingers were wet with sweat or
                                                        blood!
They stretched and strained in the darkness, and the hours
                                                crawled by like years,
Till, now, on the stroke of midnight,
        Cold, on the stroke of midnight,   60
The tip of one finger touched it! The trigger at least was hers!

writhed *twisted anxiously.*

The tip of one finger touched it. She strove no more for the rest.
Up, she stood up to attention, with the muzzle beneath her breast.
She would not risk their hearing; she would not strive again;
For the road lay bare in the moonlight;   65
        Blank and bare in the moonlight;
And the blood of her veins, in the moonlight, throbbed to her
                                                love's refrain.

Tlot-tlot; tlot-tlot! Had they heard it? The horse-hoofs ringing clear;
Tlot-tlot, tlot-tlot, in the distance! Were they deaf that they did not
                hear?
Down the ribbon of moonlight, over the brow of the hill,   70
The highwayman came riding, Riding, riding!
The red-coats looked to their priming! She stood up, straight and
                still.

looked to their priming *checked that their guns were ready to fire.*

Tlot-tlot, in the frosty silence! *Tlot-tlot,* in the echoing night!
Nearer he came and nearer. Her face was like a light.
Her eyes grew wide for a moment; she drew one last deep breath, 75
Then her finger moved in the moonlight,
    Her musket shattered the moonlight,
Shattered her breast in the moonlight and warned him – with her
                death.

He turned. He spurred to the west; he did not know who stood
Bowed, with her head o'er the musket, drenched with her own
              red blood!   80
Not till the dawn he heard it, and his face grew grey to hear
How Bess, the landlord's daughter,
    The landlord's black-eyed daughter,
Had watched for her love in the moonlight, and died in the
              darkness there.

Back, he spurred like a madman, shouting a curse to the sky,   85
With the white road smoking behind him and his rapier
              brandished high.

brandished *waved.*

Blood-red were his spurs i' the golden noon; wine-red was his
velvet coat;
When they shot him down on the highway,
    Down like a dog on the highway,
And he lay in his blood on the highway, with the bunch of lace at
             his throat.   90

      .   .   .   .

And still of a winter's night, they say, when the wind is in the trees,
When the moon is a ghostly galleon tossed upon cloudy seas,
When the road is a ribbon of moonlight over the purple moor,
A highwayman comes riding –
    Riding – riding –   95
A highwayman comes riding, up to the old inn-door.

Over the cobbles he clatters and clangs in the dark inn-yard.
And he taps with his whip on the shutters, but all is locked and barred.
He whistles a tune to the window, and who should be waiting there
But the landlord's black-eyed daughter,   100
    Bess, the landlord's daughter,
Plaiting a dark red love-knot into her long black hair.

☆

Thinking/Talking Points

▷ Consider the language of the poem.
Alfred Noyes has told a dramatic story and used exciting language to set the scene and paint the characters in the story.
Think about each of the following bits of description. What exactly does each of them make you see, hear, feel?
The wind was a *torrent of darkness; gusty trees;* The moon was a *ghostly galleon tossed upon cloudy seas;* a *ribbon* of moonlight; the *jewelled* sky; his eyes were *hollows of madness;* hair like *mouldy hay;* His face burnt *like a brand;* the *tawny* sunset; many a *sniggering* jest; she *writhed* her hands; his face *grew grey* to hear; *shouting* a curse.
Pick out some other words and phrases from the poem which you think work well.

▷ Think about the people in the story.
What impression do you have of the personalities of the highwayman, Tom the ostler, the soldiers?

▷ Do you admire the girl's behaviour? Why?/Why not?
Why did the highwayman die? How do you feel about him?

Now read through the poem again a couple of times to see what else needs thinking about before you choose your assignment.

Assignments

○ Look at the phrases we talked about in the first Thinking/Talking Point. The poet could have used more ordinary words for those in italics: 'blowing hard in the night' for 'torrent of darkness'; 'swaying' for 'gusty'; 'line' for 'ribbon', and so on, but the poem would have been much less exciting.

See if you can take the following bits from a story and make them more exciting. We've suggested an alternative to the first one.

(a) She closed the door.   *She stormed out of the room and the door shuddered on its hinges . . .*
(b) He walked down the road.
(c) The sun shone in the sky.
(d) It was raining.
(e) She was a pretty girl.
(f) The old man didn't look very friendly.
(g) I was feeling nervous.
(h) The train went quite fast.

○ Using the general shape of *The Highwayman,* write your own poem, play or short story about one of the following:
either   *The Smuggler*
  or   *The Safecracker and his girlfriend*
  or   *The Rustler*

When you have decided which story to tell, think carefully about the kind of atmosphere which would suit the hero's exploits. For example, for *The Smuggler* you might want to write about stormy seas and the dank, chill cave where he keeps his booty. For *The Safecracker*, stealthy, silent movements over the roofs in the moonlight might perhaps be accompanied by cats serenading by the dustbins, while *The Rustler*'s activities may take place in a darkness made eerie by the night noises of birds and animals, among the hot stench of cattle . . .

Begin by planning your story. For example:
1   Setting the scene
2   The smuggler leaves his girlfriend's house
3   The coastguards spot his boat leaving the bay . . .
4   The girl is questioned . . .
and so on. Limit your story to eight episodes at the most.

You may like to work on this assignment in small groups, with one person being responsible for each stage of the story, someone doing pictures, and another person organising a performance of the story when it's finished.

★

THE NAMES OF THE HARE
A version of an anonymous Middle English poem

Assignment 1

○ Jot down a dozen words and phrases to describe any animal you have watched carefully.
Think about its movement, its habits, its 'personality'.
Think about its build, its colour, its head.

Have you ever seen a hare?
How does a hare differ from a rabbit?

Here is a new version of a poem written hundreds of years ago about the hare.
Read it through a couple of times (aloud if possible) before looking at the points which follow.

The Names of the Hare

The man the hare has met
will never be the better of it
except he lay down on the land
what he carries in his hand —
be it staff or be it bow —   5
and bless him with his elbow
and come out with this litany
with devotion and sincerity
to speak the praises of the hare.
Then the man will better fare.   10

'The hare, call him scotart,
big-fellow, bouchart,
the O'Hare, the jumper,
the rascal, the racer.

Beat-the-pad, white-face,   15
funk-the-ditch, shit-ass.

The wimount, the messer,
the skidaddler, the nibbler,
the ill-met, the slabber.

The quick-scut, the dew-flirt,   20
the grass-biter, the goibert,
the home-late, the do-the-dirt.

36

1502

The starer, the wood-cat,
the purblind, the furze cat,
the skulker, the bleary-eyed,   *25*
the wall-eyed, the glance-aside
and also the hedge-springer.

The stubble-stag, the long lugs,
the stook-deer, the frisky legs,
the wild one, the skipper,   *30*
the hug-the-ground, the lurker,
the race-the-wind, the skiver,
the shag-the-hare, the hedge-squatter,
the dew-hammer, the dew-hopper,
the sit-tight, the grass-bounder,   *35*
the jig-foot, the earth-sitter,
the light-foot, the fern-sitter,
the kail-stag, the herb-cropper.

The creep-along, the sitter-still,
The pintail, the ring-the-hill,   *40*
the sudden start,
the shake-the-heart,
the belly-white,
the lambs-in-flight.

The gobshite, the gum-sucker,   *45*
the scare-the-man, the faith-breaker,
the snuff-the-ground, the baldy-skull,
(his chief name is scoundrel.)

The stag sprouting a suede horn,
the creature living in the corn,   *50*
the creature bearing all men's scorn,
the creature no one dares to name.'

When you have got all this said
then the hare's strength has been laid.
Then you might go faring forth –   *55*
east and west and south and north,
wherever you incline to go –
but only if you're skilful too.
And now, Sir Hare, good-day to you.
God guide you to a how-d'ye-do   *60*
with me: come to me dead
in either onion broth or bread.

☆

Thinking/Talking Points

▷ How many different ways of naming the hare are there in the poem?
Are there some you don't understand? Or only half-understand?
On your own or in pairs, make some suggestions for what the different names
might mean.
(Make some guesses at what strange words mean, just from their sounds.)

▷ What impression of the hare is given just by the way the poem is written out?
(e.g. Does the writing look polished or slap-dash, neat or untidy, nimble or
sluggish, serious or scatty?)

▷ Try to group the various names the hare is given around certain characteristics.
(e.g. Which phrases suggest speed/cunning/silliness?)

Read through the poem a couple more times before choosing your assignment.

Assignments

○ Write the hare's version of the poem called *The Names of the Human*.

○ Draw a series of pictures to show the different ways the hare behaves.

○ Write a similar poem of your own.
Write about a creature whose behaviour you know well (e.g. an insect, fish,
reptile, bird, tame or wild animal, brother or sister).

○ As a pair or a group, give a reading of the poem.

★

Gunn
CONSIDERING THE SNAIL

What do we mean when we talk about a 'bird's-eye view' or say 'I wish I'd been a fly on the wall'?

Do you think things look the same to a hen or to an eagle as they do to us?
Do you think a spider gets frightened/feels pain/gets excited/feels sad?
Do you think mice dream?

In this poem, Thom Gunn tries to see the world from the point of view of a snail.

Considering the Snail

The snail pushes through a green
night, for the grass is heavy
with water and meets over
the bright path he makes, where rain
has darkened the earth's dark. He   5
moves in a wood of desire,

a wood of desire a shady world of intense feelings.

pale antlers barely stirring
as he hunts. I cannot tell
what power is at work, drenched there
with purpose, knowing nothing.   10
What is a snail's fury? All
I think is that if later

drenched there with purpose singlemindedly, concentrating fully on what it's doing.

I parted the blades above
the tunnel and saw the thin
trail of broken white across   15
litter, I would never have
imagined the slow passion
to that deliberate progress.

passion strong emotion.
deliberate purposeful, slow, determined.

☆

Thinking/Talking Points

▷   How do you usually feel about snails?
Can you imagine what it would be like to be turned into one?

▷   Which phrases help us to see things from the snail's point of view?

▷   Which words describe the feelings the poet *imagines* the snail having?
What has the snail been doing to suggest it might be feeling like that?

▷   What do you think the phrase 'knowing nothing' (line 10) means?

▷   Do you think people *can* understand the way a dog or a seagull sees and feels about the world?
Did the poem make you feel differently about snails?

Assignments

○   *Considering the . . .*
Write a piece of your own, about a creature in a particular situation (e.g. a spider trapped in a bath; a fly buzzing at the window; a moth mesmerised by a flame; a dog investigating; a cat sitting, watching the world go by).
Begin by describing carefully the creature's behaviour and then try to imagine what is going on in its mind.
You may like to write as if you are the creature. If you do, think how you will help the reader guess what kind of creature you are.

○   See if you can produce a *detailed* drawing of a closely observed animal or insect.

Further reading

Ted Hughes   *Capturing Animals* (in *Poetry in the Making*)
Wodwo; Esther's Tomcat; Song of a Rat; Hawk Roosting

★

What picture does the word 'rat' suggest to you?
Jot down some words and phrases to describe as precisely as possible
(a)   a rat's appearance – its head, its tail, its body
(b)   a rat's habits and where it lives
(c)   things you associate with rats.

Write down a few words and phrases to describe your feelings as you imagine
coming across a rat – in a garden shed, maybe, or behind the dustbin.

Why do you think so many people fear rats? Why do you think some people
keep them as pets? What sort of person might be called 'a rat'?

An Advancement of Learning

I took the embankment path
(As always, deferring
The bridge). The river nosed past,
Pliable, oil-skinned, wearing

A transfer of gables and sky,   5
Hunched over the railing,
Well away from the road now, I
Considered the dirty-keeled swans.

Something slobbered curtly, close,
Smudging the silence: a rat   10
Slimed out of the water and
My throat sickened so quickly that

I turned down the path in cold sweat
But God, another was nimbling
Up the far bank, tracing its wet   15
Arcs on the stones. Incredibly then

I established a dreaded
Bridgehead. I turned to stare
With deliberate, thrilled care
At my hitherto snubbed rodent.   20

He clockworked aimlessly a while,
Stopped, back bunched and glistening,
Ears plastered down on his knobbed skull,
Insidiously listening.

deferring *deciding against,
rejecting.*

pliable *easy-going.*

gables *the triangular ends
of house walls, just beneath
the roofs.*

keeled *(literally) with keels
like boats.*
curtly *gruffly, abruptly.*

nimbling *moving nimbly,
quickly.*

arcs *curves.*

established *made.*
bridgehead *position from
which to defend oneself.*

insidiously *slyly.*

The tapered tail that followed him   25   ***tapered*** *narrowing towards*
The raindrop eye, the old snout: *the end.*
One by one I took all in.
He trained on me. I stared him out

Forgetting how I used to panic
When his grey brothers scraped and fed   30
Behind the hen-coop in our yard,
On ceiling boards above my bed.

This terror, cold, wet-furred, small-clawed,
Retreated up a pipe for sewage.
I stared a minute after him.   35
Then I walked on and crossed the bridge.

☆

Thinking/Talking Points

▷ Notice how many descriptive details the poet gives us about the place where
   this happened. Which ones help you imagine yourself there?

▷ Look at these lines:
   'Something slobbered curtly, close,
   Smudging the silence: a rat
   Slimed out of the water . . .'
   Which words help you to share the speaker's feelings?

▷ Look again at stanzas 4 and 5. What do you think the speaker found *incredible*
   about the way he reacted to the second rat?
   In your own words, say what you think was going through his mind when he
   '. . . established a dreaded/Bridgehead.'
   And what he means by '. . . deliberate, thrilled care'.

▷ Look again at stanzas 6, 7 and 9. Which details of the rat's appearance fascinate
   you? Do any of them make you see rats differently from the way you did before
   you read the poem?

▷ What does the detail '. . . I walked on and crossed the bridge' tell us?

▷ Suggest why the poem is called *An Advancement of Learning*.

Assignment

o   *An Advancement of Learning*
    Write about something dramatic which happened to you and changed the way
    you felt about something or someone. For example, perhaps you were afraid of
    someone or something just from what people had told you and when you
    encountered her/him/it for yourself, you discovered that there was nothing to
    be afraid of. Or you may have had a night-terror or superstition which you
    managed to overcome one day. Perhaps for you it wasn't rats, but heights, or
    punks, or crossing the road which made you feel uneasy. Or perhaps you had
    some prejudice which vanished when you got to know someone well.
    You may write in verse or prose.

★

Lawrence
MOSQUITO

Jot down a dozen words or phrases to describe a mosquito. Think about the creature's sound, its size, how it moves, its 'personality'. Think about how you'd feel if you heard one zinging around somewhere in the darkness of your bedroom or spotted one on the bathroom tiles.

In this poem, Lawrence chats to a mosquito.

Mosquito

When did you start your tricks,
Monsieur?

What do you stand on such high legs for?
Why this length of shredded shank,
You exaltation?   5

Is it so that you shall lift your centre of gravity upwards
And weigh no more than air as you alight upon me,
Stand upon me weightless, you phantom?

I heard a woman call you the Winged Victory
In sluggish Venice.   10
You turn your head towards your tail, and smile.

How can you put so much devilry
Into that translucent phantom shred
Of a frail corpus?

Queer, with your thin wings and your streaming legs   15
How you sail like a heron, or a dull clot of air,
A nothingness.

Yet what an aura surrounds you;
Your evil little aura, prowling, and casting a numbness on my
                                    mind.

That is your trick, your bit of filthy magic: 20
Invisibility, and the anaesthetic power
To deaden my attention in your direction.

But I know your game now, streaky sorcerer.

Queer how you stalk and prowl the air
In circles and evasions, enveloping me,   25
Ghoul on wings
Winged Victory.

shredded shank *legs which are no more than splinters.*
exaltation *long-legged creature that is thrilled with a sense of its own power.*
alight *land.*
phantom *spectre, ghost.*

sluggish *slow-moving, lazy.*

translucent *almost transparent.*
frail *feeble.*
corpus *body.*

anaesthetic *hypnotic, numbing.*

sorcerer *magician.*

stalk *hunt stealthily.*
evasions *detours made to escape.*
enveloping *surrounding.*
ghoul *demon which feeds on corpses.*

Settle, and stand on long thin shanks
Eyeing me sideways, and cunningly conscious that I am aware,
You speck.   30

I hate the way you lurch off sideways into air
Having read my thoughts against you.

Come then, let us play at unawares,
And see who wins in this sly game of bluff,
Man or mosquito.   35

You don't know that I exist, and I don't know that you exist.
Now then!

It is your trump,   *trump trumpet.*
It is your hateful little trump,
You pointed fiend,   40   *fiend devil.*
Which shakes my sudden blood to hatred of you:
It is your small, high, hateful bugle in my ear.

Why do you do it?
Surely it is bad policy.

They say you can't help it.   45

If that is so, then I believe a little in Providence protecting the   *Providence God's care.*
                                            innocent.
But it sounds so amazingly like a slogan,
A yell of triumph as you snatch my scalp.

Blood, red blood
Super-magical   50
Forbidden liquor.
                                                             *liquor rich, intoxicating
                                                             drink.*
I behold you stand
For a second enspasmed in oblivion,   *enspasmed in oblivion
Obscenely ecstasied   stupefied.
Sucking live blood,   55   *ecstasied in a state of
My blood.   perfect rapture.*

Such silence, such suspended transport,   *transport utter delight,
Such gorging,   trance, intoxication.
Such obscenity of trespass.   gorging feeding greedily.*

You stagger   60
As well as you may.
Only your accursed hairy frailty,
Your own imponderable weightlessness
Saves you, wafts you away on the very draught my anger
                                    makes in its snatching.

Away with a paean of derision,   65   *a paean of derision song
You winged blood-drop.   of triumph, mockery and
                                                            contempt.*

Can I not overtake you?
Are you one too many for me,
Winged Victory?
Am I not mosquito enough to out-mosquito you? 70

Queer, what a big stain my sucked blood makes
Besides the infinitesimal faint smear of you!
Queer, what a dim dark smudge you have disappeared into!

☆

Thinking/Talking Points

▷ Have you had feelings like the ones in Lawrence's poem?
Which of his remarks did you find surprising?

▷ How would you speak the opening two lines?
Why do you think Lawrence calls the creature 'Monsieur'? (Should it be
'Madame'?)

▷ Each of the following phrases suggests an attitude to the mosquito.
How do you picture the creature as you read each of them?
*You exaltation; you phantom; A nothingness; Ghoul on wings; Winged Victory;
You speck; You pointed fiend; winged blood-drop.*

▷ The speaker says the insect has lots of human characteristics.
See how many you can pick out.
Do you think the poet is being serious?

▷ What do you think is meant by an 'aura'?
How would you describe the *aura* of a mosquito, a snake, a slug?

▷ What is the 'sly game of bluff' that man and mosquito play? (See lines 34–37.)

▷ Describe the mosquito's state of mind after he's drunk blood. (Look at
lines 52–59.)

▷ What finally happened to the insect?
Do you think the poet respected it?
What are your own feelings about the mosquito at the end?

▷ What do you think makes something valuable?
Its size? Its strength? Its brain power? Its usefulness? The fun it gives?
Its rarity? Or what?

Read through the poem again a couple of times before choosing an assignment.

Assignments

○ Write in similar way (in verse or prose) about one of the following: a
woodlouse; a bluebottle; a wasp; a jellyfish.

○ Rewrite the poem from the mosquito's point of view. (It will probably end
differently.)

Some further reading

D.H. Lawrence   Poems: *Man and Bat; Snake*
                Essay: *Reflections on the Death of a Porcupine*

★

Read through this poem two or three times then think about the points which
follow.

Dawn Shoot

Clouds ran their wet mortar, plastered the daybreak		**mortar** *a kind of cement.*
Grey. The stones clicked tartly		**tartly** *sharply.*
If we missed the sleepers but mostly		**sleepers** *wooden supports for railway lines.*
Silent we headed up the railway		
Where now the only steam was funnelling from cows	5	
Ditched on their rumps beyond hedges,		
Cudding, watching, and knowing.		**cudding** *chewing the cud.*
The rails scored a bull's-eye into the eye		
Of a bridge. A corncrake challenged		**corncrake** *a bird with a piercing, harsh cry.*
Unexpectedly like a hoarse sentry	10	
And a snipe rocketed away on reconnaissance.		**snipe** *marshland bird with long straight bill.*
Rubber-booted, belted, tense as two parachutists,		**on reconnaissance** *spying out the land.*
We climbed the iron gate and dropped		
Into the meadow's six acres of broom, gorse and dew.		**broom** *wild shrub with bright yellow flowers.*
A sandy bank, reinforced with coiling roots,	15	
Faced you, two hundred yards from the track.		
Snug on our bellies behind a rise of dead whins,		**whins** *furze, gorse bushes.*
Our ravenous eyes getting used to the greyness,		
We settled, soon had the holes under cover.		
This was the den they all would be heading for now,	20	
Loping under ferns in dry drains, flashing		**loping** *striding.*
Brown orbits across ploughlands and grazing.		
The plaster thinned at the skyline, the whitewash		
Was bleaching on houses and stables,		
The cock would be sounding reveille	25	**reveille** *morning signal, time to get up.*
In seconds.		
And there was one breaking		
In from the gap in the corner.		

Donnelly's left hand came up
And came down on my barrel. This one was his.   *30*
'For Christ's sake', I spat, 'Take your time, there'll be more'
There was the playboy trotting up to the hole
By the ash tree, 'Wild rover no more',
Said Donnelly and emptied two barrels
And got him. I finished him off.   *35*

Another snipe catapulted into the light,
A mare whinnied and shivered her haunches
Up on the hill. The others would not be back
After three shots like that. We dandered off   **dandered** *strolled,*
to the railway; the prices were small at that time   *40*   *sauntered.*
So we did not bother to cut out the tongue.
The ones that slipped back when the all clear got round   **all clear** *signal that danger*
Would be first to examine him.   *has passed.*

Thinking/Talking Points

▷ How many wild creatures are mentioned in the poem?
Which details bring them to life?
Think about how those descriptions of birds and animals shape the way we feel about the men.

▷ Look at the first stanza again.
Notice how many separate descriptive details the poet gives us in fourteen lines.
Which details help you to imagine you are there?

▷ What do you think makes the men feel
'tense as two parachutists'?
Which other details in the poem suggest that the men imagine they are on a military exercise?

▷ Read the second stanza again.
Why 'ravenous eyes'? What sort of creature does the word suggest to you?
What creatures do you think the men are hunting?
How does the poet suggest them without naming them?

▷ Reread stanza 3.
How does the poet make us feel the passing of time?
What makes the prey's arrival startling?

▷ Look carefully at the men's conversation in stanza 4.
What words and phrases would you use to describe their personalities?

▷ What sort of creature does the word 'playboy' suggest to you?
What impact do lines 34–35 have on you?
See if you can explain why.

▷ Look at the final stanza again.
How do you think the men felt about what they'd done?
Do you think the poet's attitude is the same as theirs?
Give reasons for your answers.

Before choosing your assignment, read through the poem again a couple of times to see what else deserves attention. Are there any words or phrases you don't understand? Are there any interesting details you hadn't notice before?

Assignments

○ Essay: 'Without making any direct criticism, *Dawn Shoot* is a powerful protest against our wanton destruction of wildlife.' Do you agree? Look closely at the way the poet has shaped the way we see the incident.

○ *First Blood*
Write an account, in verse or prose, imaginary or based upon something which happened to you, of someone's first experience of the killing of an animal (e.g. for 'sport'; on a farm; in a slaughterhouse; in a religious ceremony, or through somebody's carelessness).

○ Compare Heaney's poem with this one by John Stallworthy.
Which poem do you like best? Why?
Refer to the particular details in each poem which you find most/least colourful and dramatic.

First Blood

It was. The breech smelling of oil,
The stock of resin – buried snug
In the shoulder. Not too much recoil
At the firing of the first slug

(Jubilantly into the air)   5
Not yet too little. Targets pinned
Against a tree: shot down: and there
Abandoned to the sniping wind.

My turn first to carry the gun.
Indian file and camouflaged   10
With contours of green shade and sun
We ghosted between larch and larch.

A movement between branches – thump
Of a fallen cone. The barrel
Jumps, making branches jump   15
Higher, dislodging the squirrel

To the next tree. Your turn, my turn.
The silhouette retracts its head.
A hit. 'Let's go back to the lawn.'
'We can't leave it carrying lead   20

For the rest of its life. Reload.
Finish him off. Reload again.'
It was now *him*, and when he showed
The sky cracked like a window pane.

He broke away: traversed a full   *25*
Half dozen trees: vanished. Had found
A hole? We watched that terrible
Slow spiral to the clubbing ground.

His back was to the tree. His eyes
Were gun barrels. He was dumb,   *30*
And we could not see past the size
Of his hands or hear for the drum

In his side. Four shots point-blank
To dull his eyes, a fifth to stop
The shiver in his clotted flank,   *35*
A fling of earth. As we stood up

The larches closed their ranks. And when
Earth would not muffle the drumming blood
We, like dishonoured soldiers, ran
The gauntlet of a darkening wood.   *40*

★

WHEN I WENT
TO THE CIRCUS

Have you ever *seen* a circus? Have you ever *been* to one?
Why do you think circuses are less popular today than they used to be?

Have you ever been to the theatre, to a concert, or a sports event?
What do you remember most vividly?
How would watching a video of the event be different from being there?

Why do you think people sometimes find 'live' shows disappointing
when they are used to watching things on television or listening to music
only on tape or disc?

Read through this poem two or three times before thinking about the
points which follow.

When I Went to the Circus

When I went to the circus that had pitched on the waste lot   ***pitched*** *set up its Big Top.*
it was full of uneasy people
frightened of the bare earth and the temporary canvas
and the smell of horses and other beasts
instead of merely the smell of man.   5

Monkeys rode rather grey and wizened   ***wizened*** *like little old men,*
on curly plump piebald ponies   *wrinkled, dried up.*
and the children uttered a little cry –   ***piebald*** *light in colour with*
and dogs jumped through hoops and turned somersaults   *irregular markings.*
and then the geese scuttled in in a little flock   10
and round the ring they went to the sound of the whip
then doubled, and back, with a funny up-flutter of wings –
and the children suddenly shouted out.

Then came the hush again, like a hush of fear.

The tight-rope lady, pink and blonde and nude-looking, with a
               few gold spangles   15   ***spangles*** *glittering*
footed cautiously out on the rope, turned prettily, spun round   *decorations.*
bowed, and lifted her foot in her hand, smiled, swung her parasol   ***parasol*** *umbrella.*
to another balance, tripped round, poised, and slowly sank   ***poised*** *held her position*
her handsome thighs down, down, till she slept her splendid body   *carefully, gracefully.*
               on the rope.
When she rose, tilting her parasol, and smiled at the cautious
               people   20
they cheered, but nervously.

The trapeze man, slim and beautiful and like a fish in the air
swung great curves through the upper space, and came down like
                                a star.
– And the people applauded, with hollow, frightened applause.

The elephants, huge and grey, loomed their curved bulk through
                          the dusk   25
and sat up, taking strange postures, showing the pink soles of   **postures** *stances, poses.*
                           their feet
and curling their precious live trunks like ammonites   **ammonites** *spiral fossil*
and moving always with soft slow precision   *shells.*
as when a great ship moves to anchor.
The people watched and wondered, and seemed to resent the
                    mystery that lies in beasts.   30

Horses, gay horses, swirling round and plaiting   **plaiting** *weaving in and*
in a long line, their heads laid over each other's necks;   *out of each other.*
they were happy, they enjoyed it;
all the creatures seemed to enjoy the game
in the circus, with their circus people.   35

But the audience, compelled to wonder   **compelled** *forced.*
compelled to admire the bright rhythms of moving bodies
compelled to see the delicate skill of flickering human bodies
flesh flamey and a little heroic, even in a tumbling clown,
they were not really happy.   40
There was no gushing response, as there is at the film.

When modern people see the carnal body dauntless and flickering   **carnal** *sensual,*
gay playing among the elements neatly, beyond competition   *unrestrained.*
and displaying no personality,   **dauntless** *bold, fearless.*
modern people are depressed.   45   **playing among the**
                                                                   elements neatly
Modern people feel themselves at a disadvantage.   *performing in an easy,*
They know they have no bodies that could play among the   *unselfconscious, primitive*
                                elements.   *way whether in the air, in*
They have only their personalities, that are best seen flat, on the   *the water, on the ground or*
                                film,   *through fire.*
flat personalities in two dimensions, imponderable and touchless.   **imponderable** *weightless,*
                                        unreal.
And they grudge the circus people the swooping gay weight of
                            limbs   50
that flower in mere movement,
and they grudge them the immediate, physical understanding they
                    have with their circus beasts,
and they grudge them their circus life altogether.

Yet the strange, almost frightened shout of delight that comes now
                    and then from the children
shows that the children vaguely know how cheated they are of
                    their birthright   55   **birthright** *their rights as*
in the bright wild circus flesh.   *human beings.*

               ☆

Thinking/Talking Points

▷ Which details show this is a 'live' performance?
Why do you think the audience feels 'uneasy'?

▷ Which details tell us that this circus isn't glamorous?

▷ What do you notice about the different ways the grown-ups and the children behaved?
How would you explain that?

▷ How did the speaker feel about the various acts?
Describe his attitude to the circus people.

▷ 'There was no gushing response, as there is at the film.'
What do you think 'gushing' means here?

▷ Look again at lines 42–49.
What do you think the speaker means by 'personality' here?
And what does he mean when he says 'modern people' have 'flat personalities'? (Think what we mean by 'a TV personality'.)

Read through the poem again a couple of times to see if there are any words or phrases you don't fully understand or any interesting details you hadn't noticed before.

Assignments

○ *When I Went to . . .*
Write an account, in verse or prose, of any experience you've had of a live performance (e.g. a play; a concert; dancing; a pantomime; a fireworks display; a sports event; or a circus).
Bring out the special flavour of the occasion: the atmosphere, the smells, the noises, the distractions, which were all part of the show.
What did the audience add to the show?
Were you disappointed by anything?

○ Essay: Do you think life would be less exciting if entertainment came only from records, films and television?
Discuss any experiences you have had of live and 'canned' entertainment.
Bring out what made them so different.

★

Hopkins
THE WINDHOVER

You are out walking in the early morning.
Suddenly, you spot a bird in flight. See if you can identify it.
Imagine the lines it might paint on the air: what shapes? what colours?
Think of the movements its wings make.

Now imagine yourself as the bird.
Picture what you see as you soar into the air and then swoop.
Think what it might feel like as the wind pressed against your feathers . . .
And then imagine the wind carrying you forwards and upwards.

Write down as many words and phrases as you can to describe a bird's flight
(a)   as it appears to an observer on earth, and
(b)   as you imagine it from the bird's point of view.
Write down some words to describe how each might be feeling.

On the opposite page is a poem about a kestrel. Read it a few times and then try
reading it out loud to yourself or to a partner.
Do not worry too much about the meaning of unfamiliar words: concentrate
upon the sound and rhythm of the poem. See if you can *feel* what the poet is
saying before you can *understand* how he is saying it.

When you have read the poem aloud a few times (and, if possible, listened to
others reading it), consider the points which follow.

Thinking/Talking Points

▷   Did reading the poem aloud make you feel the poet's mood even though there
were bits you didn't understand?
How would you describe his mood?
Which words suggest that mood?

▷   Pick out three or four phrases which you find it difficult to 'explain'.
(a)   What does the sound of the words suggest to you?
(b)   Use the glossary and a dictionary to see how many different meanings
each word can have. (Use something bigger than a pocket dictionary if
possible.)
(c)   Work in pairs to see if you can come up with some sort of explanation for
the phrases that you found mysterious.

▷   Suggest why the poem is dedicated *To Christ our Lord*.

▷   Do you think Windhover or Kestrel is the better name for the bird? Why?

Read through the poem again now, several times, preferably aloud. Which
phrases do you still find mysterious? Is that a bad thing?

The Windhover

To Christ our Lord

I caught this morning morning's minion, king-
  dom of daylight's dauphin, dapple-dawn-drawn Falcon, in his riding
  Of the rolling level underneath him steady air, and striding
High there, how he rung upon the rein of a wimpling wing
In his ecstasy! then off, off forth on swing,
  As a skate's heel sweeps smooth on a bow-bend: the hurl and gliding
  Rebuffed the big wind. My heart in hiding
Stirred for a bird, – the achieve of, the mastery of the thing!

Brute beauty and valour and act, oh, air, pride, plume, here
  Buckle! AND the fire that breaks from thee then, a billion
Times told lovelier, more dangerous. O my chevalier!

No wonder of it: shéer plód makes plough down sillion
Shine, and blue-bleak embers, ah my dear,
  Fall, gall themselves, and gash gold-vermilion.

caught *caught sight of.*
morning's minion *the morning's darling, favourite.*
dauphin *prince, heir-apparent.*
dapple *mixture of colours.*
rung up on the rein of a wimpling wing *quivered his wings, hovered as if held by the wind.*

ecstasy *joy, delight.*
bow-bend *arc.*
rebuffed *resisted; shoved back.*
achieve *achievement.*
brute *like a wild animal.*
valour *courage.*
plume *plumage.*
buckle *come together.*
chevalier *champion, hero.*

plod *dull, repetitive, hard work.*
sillion *a strip of farm land.*
shine *the rusty ploughshare shines after use.*
embers *dying fuel in a fire.*
gall themselves . . . gash *knock, wound themselves; as the embers in a dying fire fall, a brilliant glowing wound is revealed.*

Assignments

○ In pairs or a small group, work on a performance of *The Windhover*.
Think about different ways of dividing the lines/individual words between one or more voices. Think carefully about tempo: where will you speed up, where slow down? Think about variations of tone and volume. Which words will you stress? In what mood will the poem open and close? Think about the various voice sounds which might be used to accompany the reading.

○ See if you can produce a drawing/painting/collage to express in some way the feelings generated by the poem.

○ Write a piece in which you attempt to 'catch' one of the following: a wild horse; a cat playing with a bird; sunrise; the experience of skiing/diving/dancing/sprinting/fighting.

★

Joseph
IN MEMORY OF GOD

What do you understand by the word 'conservation'?
Sometimes when there are plans to build a new airport or an extra stretch of
motorway, some people will object that the construction will destroy the
habitat of a rare bird or a wild flower or will spoil an area of 'outstanding
natural beauty'.
How do you feel about such arguments?
Look at the choices below:
>   a new Disneyland *or* keeping a bird sanctuary
>   a dry ski-slope *or* leaving untouched a field where wild orchids
>   occasionally bloom
>   a quicker route to the city *or* preserving the nesting site of a rare species of
>   wild duck
What are some of the arguments you can imagine for and against the new
project?

Assignment 1

○ Prepare a short speech in favour of or against a proposal in your area to
   demolish a rarely-used church and to build a hypermarket in its place.

Read through this poem a couple of times, making a note of the two attitudes
to conservation which you think are being presented.

In memory of God

I suppose they would've shot the moon down,
If they could have, into little pieces,
To make a new one
Even while saying isn't it strange, isn't it beautiful

Come, I will show you a marvel   5
Of man.

There on the green
A huge contraption in a palisade.   *contraption* complicated
'You have here a perfect replica of a whale.   *structure.*
Every branch of knowledge known to man   10 *palisade* fence.
(You name it, we got it) has gone into this project   *replica* model.
To bring you the fabulous wonders of the deep.'

deep ocean.

56

Yes, here's a panel
That tells you who gave grants for what to whom
And who the electrician was, and which boroughs   15   *a penny rate* a local tax.
Raised a penny rate to send the team
To find the stuff to make the eyes – etcetera.
'Ask him not to touch, lady, would you mind? –
Just to look at, son, so you know what they looked like –
We need a grant for a pool, and another two thou to get it   20   *two thou* £2000.
Buoyant, so it would *move*. Then there's maintenance.'   *buoyant* floating.
                                                                       maintenance upkeep.
                                                                       perpetual everlasting.
Far in perpetual waters a creature turned
Coasted and turned in perfect machinations   *machinations* movements.
Moving, like clouds at the edge of the world, untended   *untended* with nobody
Simply itself in its extraordinary being: 25   looking after it.
Easy, so easy moving through the water.

Stupid men. All you had to do
To get a whale, was not to spend one penny, not do anything
But let be what miraculously was there.

No one on earth can make a whale again.   30
And when, because of what you have made way for
The rats over-run us, think of the mild wonders
We could have let keep the world:
Unclever, not like us, yet much more skilful
And useful, alas, in all their parts to man.   35

But being no use would probably not have saved you:
The strange shining disc that lights you to your extinction   *extinction* death of the
Far over your dark pathways,   species.
And even whatever caused the moon's pull, the life of waters
To maintain the whale –   40
They would put it in their pocket if they could.

☆

Thinking/Talking Points

▷   How would you describe the tone of voice of the speaker?
     Which phrases in the poem bring out her mood most clearly?

▷   According to the speaker, what is silly about this project to make a replica of a
     whale?

▷   Can you think of other creatures which might soon be known only as
     photographs or plastic models in museums?

▷   What impression of the living whale does stanza 5 give you?
     Which phrases do you find most vivid?

▷   'Unclever, not like us, yet much more skilful'
     (a)   See if you can explain this in your own way.
     (b)   Do you think the speaker is correct in this description of whales?
     (c)   What other creatures do you think might be described like this?

57

▷ Why was it a pity that whales were 'useful . . . in all their parts to man'?

▷ Which lines of the poem relate to its title?
What is the poet saying about men's attitude to God?

▷ Can you think of two meanings for the poem's last line?

Assignment 2

○ *Spare the Species!*
A highly advanced, super-intelligent, and very powerful race of creatures
invades Earth. After careful consideration, they have decided that humans are
a waste of space and precious resources: they can't master Lingo (the new
Earth language), can perform only a few simple, charming but unprofitable
tricks (such as painting pictures, making music, dancing), need lots of
expensive medical facilities to keep them alive, and the amount of food they
consume is out of all proportion to their productivity – the simplest machines
can produce twice as much at a thousandth of the cost.
You have been elected Spokesperson for the Human Race. You have five
minutes to convince the Central Committee for Efficiency and Progress that
humans are worth keeping alive.
You may present your case as a speech, an essay or a poem.

○ Essay: *All Things Bright and Beautiful*
Do you believe that the usefulness, the profitability, the popularity of
something is the most important consideration when we have to decide what
to keep, what to destroy?
There are many 'reasons' why the things listed below could disappear before
long to make way for 'progress' and 'efficiency'. Choose one of them and see
what arguments you can come up with for and against conserving them.
Do you think the world would be a poorer place if such things disappeared?

    The Green Belt and/or common land
    whales/tigers/elephants/eagles/nightingales
    rare species of flowers or butterflies or insects
    art galleries, museums and/or libraries
    bird sanctuaries
    cathedrals
    parks
    stretches of coastline where there are no marinas, caravan sites or
    'amusements'.

★

Think of a dozen words to describe mushrooms.

Where do they grow? How do they grow? When?
What are the colours of mushrooms?
How would you describe their textures, taste and smell?

If mushrooms talked, what do you think their voices would be like?
If you were making a cartoon film, what sort of personalities would you give
mushrooms: bold; shy; fierce; sly; friendly; cold; intelligent; dumb?

Here's how Sylvia Plath imagines them.

Mushrooms

Overnight, very
Whitely, discreetly,   **discreetly** *cautiously,*
Very quietly   *secretively.*

Our toes, our noses
Take hold on the loam,   5   **loam** *earth.*
Acquire the air.

Nobody sees us,
Stops us, betrays us;   **betrays us** *gives us away.*
The small grains make room.

Soft fists insist on   10
Heaving the needles,   **needles** *fir or pine needles.*
The leafy bedding,

Even the paving,
Our hammers, our rams,
Earless and eyeless,   15

Perfectly voiceless,
Widen the crannies,   **crannies** *chinks, gaps.*
Shoulder through holes. We

Diet on water,
On crumbs of shadow,   20
Bland-mannered, asking   **bland-mannered**
                                         behaving very politely,
Little or nothing,   *unassumingly.*
So many of us!
So many of us!

We are shelves, we are   25
Tables, we are meek,   **meek** *humble, timid.*
We are edible,   **are edible** *can be eaten.*

Nudgers and shovers
In spite of ourselves.
Our kind multiplies: 30   **kind** *sort.*

We shall by morning
Inherit the earth,   **inherit** *take over.*
Our foot's in the door.

☆

Thinking/Talking Points

▷ How do
(a)   the way the poem is written out and
(b)   the rhythm of the poem
suggest the mushrooms' personality?

▷ In what sort of voice would you read the poem (e.g. loud; quiet; sly; ghostly; nervous; bold; sinister)?
Try reading a few lines in different kinds of voice.

▷ Jot down some words of your own to describe these mushrooms.

▷ What does the phrase
'Soft fists insist' (line 10)
suggest to you about the mushrooms' personalities?

▷ 'Earless and eyeless,
Perfectly voiceless'
How do these details make you feel?

▷ Were there other details in the poem which surprised or amused you?

Now read the poem again a few times,
Listen to the sounds of the words.

Assignments

○ Draw a series of cartoons to illustrate *Mushrooms*.

○ Compose a similar piece, in verse or prose, about one of these:
moths; clouds; poppies; fog; slugs; frost; snow; thistles.

You may like to see if you can write a poem of exactly the same length as *Mushrooms*. Pay careful attention to the *sounds* of your words.

★

Storms

How do you feel if you wake up in the middle of a thunderstorm?
What things do the noises of storms make you imagine?

Have you ever found yourself far from shelter when a storm broke?
See how many precise details of the event you can recall.

Imagine you were painting a storm.
What colours would you use? What kinds of brush-stroke?

Imagine making music to accompany a storm in a film.
What noises would you try to imitate?
How fast or slow would you make the music?

What human moods do you associate with storms?

Assignment 1

○   It is midnight.
You are sitting in a cosy place, listening to a storm raging outside.
Describe the sounds you hear, the movements you imagine.
Describe how the storm makes you feel.
There is a phone call. You have to go out into the storm.
Describe what you see, hear, feel as you battle against the weather.

Assignment 2

○   Here is a poem about a night followed by a day of tremendous bluster.
We have taken out some key words – you will find them listed below the
poem. They are not listed in the proper order.
Singly or in pairs, suggest which word fits each gap best.
You will need to try out some words in different places before finding the best
slots for them.
Each word may be used only once!

A dictionary would be handy for this assignment.

Wind

This house has been far out at . . . all night,
The woods . . . through darkness, the . . . hills,
Winds . . . the fields under the window
Floundering black astride and blinding wet

floundering *struggling clumsily.*

Till day rose; then under an . . . sky   5
The hills had new places, and wind wielded
Blade-light, luminous black and emerald,
. . . like the lens of a mad eye.

wind wielded *thrust like a sword by the wind.*
luminous *bright, glowing.*

At noon I . . . along the house-side as far as
The coal-house door, I dared once to look up –   10
Through the brunt wind that dented the balls of my eyes
The tent of the hills drummed and . . . its guy-rope,

brunt *violent.*

The fields . . . , the skyline a grimace,
At any second to bang and vanish with a flap:
The wind . . . a magpie away and a black-   15
Back gull bent like an . . . bar slowly. The house

grimace *snarl, frown.*

. . . like some fine green goblet in the note
That any second would . . . it. Now deep
In chairs, in front of the great fire, we grip
Our hearts and cannot entertain book, thought,   20

entertain book *settle to reading.*

Or each other. We watch the fire . . . ,
And feel the roots of the house move, but sit on,
Seeing the window . . . to come in,
Hearing the stones . . . out under the horizons.

☆

Here are the words that we have taken out:

tremble	shatter	sea	stampeding
strained	blazing	scaled	flung
quivering	crashing	rang	flexing
iron	booming	orange	cry

Here is another poem, this time about a thunderstorm.
Which words and phrases do you think describe the lightning best?

Storm in the Black Forest

Now it is almost night, from the bronzey soft sky
jugfull after jugfull of pure white liquid fire, bright white
tipples over and spills down,
and is gone
and gold-bronze flutters through the thick upper air.   5

And as the electric liquid pours out, sometimes
a still brighter white snake wriggles among it, spilled
and tumbling wriggling down the sky:
and then the heavens cackle with uncouth sounds.

cackle laugh hoarsely like old women.

And the rain won't come, the rain refuses to come!   10

uncouth rough, coarse.

This is the electricity that man is supposed to have mastered
chained, subjugated to his use!

subjugated tamed.

supposed to!

☆

Assignment 3

o   Draw or paint a picture to illustrate one of the poems.

o   Write a piece of your own capturing the mood of one of these:
a blizzard; a storm at sea; a forest fire; a flood; an avalanche; an earthquake.
A thesaurus would be handy for this assignment.
Begin by collecting together as many dramatic words as you can to describe the
movements you imagine, e.g. shoving; boiling; swirling; tumbling.
Then find lots of words to describe the noises, e.g. growling; grinding;
gnashing; smashing.
Think about the colours and shapes of things when they get caught up in a
storm or fire, e.g. twisted; crippled; crumpling; dissolving.
Try to imagine how your body would feel as you tried to get away from the
disaster.

Some other storm poems

Ted Hughes	*October Dawn; November; Rain*
Theodore Roethke	*Big Wind*
John Donne	*The Storm*
Allen Curnow	*Wild Iron*

★

Gibson
FLANNAN ISLE

Here is a mystery story.
Read through the poem a couple of times and then think about the points
which follow.

Flannan Isle

'Though three men dwelt on Flannan Isle
To keep the lamp alight,
As we steered under the lee, we caught
No glimmer through the night.'

A passing ship at dawn had brought   5
The news; and quickly we set sail,
To find out what strange thing might ail
The keepers of the deep-sea light.

The Winter day broke blue and bright,
With glancing sun and glancing spray,   10
While o'er the swell our boat made way,
As gallant as a gull in flight.

But as we neared the lonely Isle,
And looked up at the naked height,
And saw the lighthouse towering white,   15
With blinded lantern, that all night
Had never shot a spark
Of comfort through the dark,
So ghostly in the cold sunlight
It seemed, that we were struck the while   20
With wonder all too dread for words.

And as into the tiny creek
We stole beneath the hanging crag,
We saw three queer, black ugly birds –
Too big, by far, in my belief,   25
For cormorant or shag –
Like seamen sitting bolt-upright
Upon a half-tide reef:
But, as we neared, they plunged from sight,
Without a sound, or spurt of white.   30

the lee side that is sheltered
from the wind.

ail trouble.

swell waves.
gallant noble, fine-looking.

cormorant large greedy
sea-bird.
shag crested cormorant.
reef ridge of rocks or sand
just below the surface of the
sea.

And still too mazed to speak,
We landed; and made fast the boat;
And climbed the track in single file,
Each wishing he were safe afloat,
On any sea, however far,   35
So it be far from Flannan Isle:
And still we seemed to climb, and climb
As though we'd lost all count of time,
And so must climb for evermore.
Yet, all too soon, we reached the door,   40
The black, sun-blistered lighthouse-door,
That gapcd for us ajar.

As, on the threshold, for a spell,
We paused, we seemed to breathe the smell
Of limewash and of tar,   45
Familiar as our daily breath,
As though 'twere some strange scent of death:
And so, yet wondering, side by side,
We stood a moment, still tongue-tied:
And each with black foreboding eyed   50
The door, ere we should fling it wide,
To leave the sunlight for the gloom:
Till, plucking courage up, at last,
Hard on each other's heels we passed,
Into the living-room.   55

Yet, as we crowded through the door,
We only saw a table, spread
For dinner, meat and cheese and bread;
But, all untouched; and no one there;
As though, when they sat down to eat,   60
Ere they could even taste,
Alarm had come; and they in haste
Had risen and left the bread and meat:
For at the table-head a chair
Lay tumbled on the floor.   65

We listened; but we only heard
The feeble chirping of a bird
That starved upon its perch;
And, listening still, without a word,
We set about our hopeless search.   70

We hunted high, we hunted low;
And soon ransacked the empty house;
Then o'er the Island, to and fro,
We ranged, to listen and to look
In every cranny, cleft or nook   75
That might have hid a bird or mouse:
But, though we searched from shore to shore

made fast tied up.

threshold entrance, doorway.

foreboding having a sense of approaching evil.

ransacked searched thoroughly.
ranged roamed, wandered.
cranny chink, small hole.
cleft crack in rock.
nook narrow corner, comfortable sheltered spot, isolated place.

We found no sign in any place:
And soon again stood face to face
Before the gaping door: 80
And stole into the room once more
As frightened children steal.
Ay: though we hunted high and low,
And hunted everywhere,
Of the three men's fate we found no trace   85
Of any kind in any place,
But a door ajar, and an untouched meal,
And an overtoppled chair.

And as we listened in the gloom
Of that forsaken living-room –   90
A chill clutch on our breath –
We thought how ill-chance came to all
Who kept the Flannan Light:
And how the rock had been the death
Of many a likely lad: 95
How six had come to a sudden end,
And three had gone stark mad:
And one whom we'd all known as a friend
Had leapt from the lantern one still night,
And fallen dead by the lighthouse wall: 100
And long we thought
On the three we sought,
And of what might yet befall.

Like curs a glance has brought to heel,
We listened flinching there: 105
And looked, and looked, on the untouched meal,
And the overtoppled chair.

We seemed to stand for an endless while,
Though still no word was said,
Three men alive on Flannan Isle,   110
Who thought on three men dead.

☆

stole/steal crept/creep.

forsaken abandoned, deserted.

ill-chance bad luck.

stark completely.

sought looked for.
befall happen.

cur mongrel, snappy bad-tempered dog.
flinching drawing back in fear.

Thinking/Talking Points

▷ Jot down some words of your own to describe the mood of the first twenty lines.
Which particular words and phrases in the poem do most to create the atmosphere?

▷ Imagine you are one of the three men arriving on Flannan Isle.
Describe your feelings as you approach the island.

▷ Can you explain the presence of the
'three queer, black ugly birds'?
Have you any idea how or why they managed to plunge into the water
'Without a sound, or spurt of white'?

▷ What do the men find on Flannan Isle to make them feel uneasy?
Suggest what might have happened to the three lighthouse-keepers.

▷ Look again at lines 92 to 100.
What do we learn about the fates of previous lighthouse-keepers?
Can you suggest why they all suffered as they did?

▷ What do you think is going through the minds of the three men who have just arrived on the island as they think
'of what might yet befall'?

Assignments

○ *A Journey to Flannan Isle*
You are one of the men who has been sent to search the island.
Tell your story from the beginning of your journey. Base your work around the poem but add plenty of details of your own.
Bring out your feelings and the characters of your companions.
How the story ends is up to you!

○ As a series of diary entries, tell the story of one of the previous lighthouse-keepers.
Begin by making everything on the island seem normal.
Gradually include more and more uncanny details.
Are these things really happening or is the loneliness of the place affecting the writer's mind?

○ *Unsolved Mystery of Flannan Isle*
You are a newspaper reporter sent to investigate the latest disappearance on Flannan Isle.
Where do you begin your enquiries?
Whom, if anybody, do you find to interview?
Perhaps you come across people who have lost relatives on the isle.
What do you discover as you explore the old lighthouse?
Do you find any solution to the mystery?
Present your story in the form of a newspaper front page.

★

from THE WRECK OF THE DEUTSCHLAND

The Voyage and Stranding
of the *Deutschland**

Setting out from Bremen to New York on Saturday, 4 December 1875, the
Deutschland, after anchoring overnight near Bremerhaven at the mouth of
the Weser, thrust into the North Sea and headed west, urged by heavy
winds and squalls of snow. The officers were not worried. The *Deutschland*
was a solid British-built iron ship over 300 feet long with five bulkheads, its
single screw driven by powerful 600 horse-power engines. The German
company to which the ship belonged had run a regular transatlantic service
to New York since 1857 without losing a single life, and on board there
were in addition to the Master of the ship, Captain Brickenstein, five officers
with Masters' certificates and three river pilots. Over-confident of their
'mastery' of the elements and pleased to have a following gale, they used
their foretopsail to increase their speed, although the air was too thick with
haze and snow to allow them to check their position by observation. The
complicated set of the tidal currents in the North Sea, of which none had a
proper *mastery*, should have made them more cautious, especially when in
the total obscurity of snow-blinded night they entered the region of deadly
sandbanks off the mouth of the Thames, where hundreds of ships were
destroyed every year.

Because of a trade depression the *Deutschland* had sailed without a full
cargo and with only a sixth of her peak passenger complement on board.
Exact figures were never established, but there were fortunately only about
a hundred and thirteen passengers – settlers returning to America, along
with some new settlers, including the five nuns. As they lay asleep or ill
from the violent tossing, the ship, running before the storm with engines at
full speed, drove in the dark towards the unknown. Only when soundings
gave results at variance with their dead reckoning did the Master order the
speed reduced. Too late there was a cry of 'Breakers ahead!', but reversing
the engines shattered the propeller, leaving the ship to lurch broadside onto
a submerged sandbank.

The North Sea in the fury of a gale generates some of the highest waves
which have ever been measured. Huge breakers cascaded over the ship,
lifting her and slamming her down, yard by yard further onto the bank.
Rockets were fired as distress signals, but their man-made lightning was
swallowed by the snowstorm. The surges swamped and smashed two
lifeboats, and snapping three-inch ropes like thread, snatched a third from
its davits, and tossed it into the confused currents with three men clinging
aboard, on a nightmare voyage which was to last thirty-six hours and to
cost two of them their lives. Meanwhile no further attempts to abandon

* From Mackenzie: *A Reader's Guide to Gerard Manley Hopkins* (Thames and Hudson)

ship were made. When Monday's daylight at last penetrated the pall of clouds, the officers realized that their ship was embedded on the Kentish Knock, a great bank about seven miles long, one of a series of treacherous underwater sand ranges near the mouth of the Thames which run parallel to the east coast. Harwich, the nearest port from which help could be hoped for, lay beyond the horizon, separated from them by banks and shoals difficult to evade even in better light and less tumult.

The ship fought magnificently for her life, enduring the pounding of the seas hour after hour without breaking up. Rescue seemed momentarily at hand. A lightship saw her distress and fired carronades whose flash could occasionally be glimpsed though the roar of the surf drowned their reports. Several ships appeared to be heading to help them, then veered away; not from callousness, as the shipwrecked imagined, but because they were themselves in peril and the stranded vessel was inaccessible among the pounding waves. Ten hours dragged by before distress-rockets, seen after much delay and repeated by intermediate lightships, eventually alerted the coastguards at Harwich. By that time a second night of fury had begun. The would-be rescuers ashore knew only that somewhere among the sea-tormented sand-banks there was a vessel in need, but her whereabouts or actual predicament they had no means of guessing. To have battled their way out into the darkness to investigate would have been suicidal.

As the tide rose and leaks between the strained timbers outpaced the pumps, the passengers were driven from the lower decks of the steerage and intermediate saloon to the first class. Then the first saloon became awash, and in the early hours of Tuesday male passengers were ordered into the rigging, while the women and children clambered on to the long table below the skylight. Finally they too were in danger of being drowned and the stewardess led them up the companion-way to the deck. But a great wave catching the stewardess and almost sweeping her overboard, the nuns (with some other women) returned to the saloon and their prayers. One woman hanged herself, and a man committed suicide by cutting a vein. The tallest of the five nuns, thrusting her head through the skylight, could be heard above the storm calling to God to come quickly. Some of the survivors found her call as unnerving as the cry of a woman from the wheel-house, 'My child is drowned, my little one, Adam!' Many of those in the rigging, drenched with spray and numbed by the gale, fell to the deck or into the icy waves. By the time Tuesday's dawn broke at last and the subsiding tide left the deck relatively dry, some sixty of the passengers and crew, including all five of the nuns, had died, over a quarter of those who had embarked. Shortly after 10.30 am a tug, which had set out from Harwich the moment it was light enough to locate them, at last arrived – about thirty hours after their stranding – and carried the survivors back to safety.

☆

Assignment

This is an activity for which a thesaurus and a large dictionary would be handy.

○ Working singly or in pairs, choose just one moment from the shipwreck (e.g. the lifeboat with three men aboard plunging into the raging waters; the moment when the *Deutschland* crashed onto the Kentish Knock; a time when another ship seemed to be coming to the rescue; your attempt to climb the rigging; when the nun or the mother began to call out).

Begin by seeing, trying to hear, to feel the scene in your imagination: the kinds of movements the ship would be making under the surging, buffeting, pounding, exploding waves; how it would feel to lurch so violently, unceasingly and be thrown, battered about.

Picture just one person's face lit by a flash of lightning.

Imagine the eyes, the mouth, the hair.

Imagine bits of the ship being torn apart by the tempest.

Try to see just two or three details in close-up: the whipping of the rigging, for example, or the groaning, tearing, splintering of timbers.

Now make a picture-in-words of that episode, in verse or prose. Choose words to dramatise:

> the thundering violence of the storm
> the terror of passengers and crew
> the chaos, the confusion
> above all, the stupendous noise and wild hurling of the ordeal.

You may like to see if you can combine your versions of different moments into a larger work – perhaps for a wall display or a recording.

Here is an extract from the poem Hopkins wrote immediately after he read about the wreck.

Read it through several times, experimenting with ways of reading it aloud if possible. Do not worry that there are bits which you do not understand. See if you can feel the movement, the energy of the writing.

from **The Wreck of the *Deutschland***
Part the Second

11

'Some find me a sword; some
    The flange and the rail; flame,
Fang, or flood' goes Death on drum,
    And storms bugle his fame.
But we dream we are rooted in earth – Dust!   5
Flesh falls within sight of us, we, though our flower the same,
    Wave with the meadow, forget that there must
The sour scythe cringe, and the blear share come.

find me get to know me as.
flange and the rail the wheel of a railway train running along the track.
fang a wild animal's tooth.
bugle broadcast.
dream imagine.
Dust really, we are nothing but dust.
forget we forget.
scythe a long curved knife used to cut corn.
blear share blind, indiscriminate ploughshare.

72

On Saturday sailed from Bremen,
　　American-outward-bound,
Take settler and seamen, tell men with women,
　　Two hundred souls in the round –
O Father, not under thy feathers nor ever as guessing
The goal was a shoal, of a fourth the doom to be drowned;
　　Yet did the dark side of the bay of thy blessing
Not vault them, the million of rounds of thy mercy not reeve
　　　　　　　　　　　　　even them in?

10

15

tell count.
in the round in round numbers.
Father God.
goal end of the journey.
shoal submerged sandbank.
a fourth a quarter.
vault cover, protect.
reeve fasten, make safe.

13

Into the snows she sweeps,
　　Hurling the haven behind,
The Deutschland, on Sunday; and so the sky keeps,
　　For the infinite air is unkind,
And the sea flint-flake, black-backed in the regular blow,
Sitting Eastnortheast, in cursed quarter, the wind;
　　Wiry and white-fiery and whirlwind-swivelled snow
Spins to the widow-making unchilding unfathering deeps.

20

hurling thrusting.
haven safe anchorage.
keeps stays.

deeps ocean.

14

She drove in the dark to leeward,
　　She struck – not a reef or a rock
But the combs of a smother of sand: night drew her
　　Dead to the Kentish Knock;
And she beat the bank down with her bows and the ride of
　　　　　　　　　　　　　her keel:
The breakers rolled on her beam with ruinous shock;
　　And canvas and compass, the whorl and the wheel
Idle for ever to waft her or wind her with, these she endured.

25

30

leeward to the sheltered side.

dead helpless; precisely on course.

keel spine of the ship.
breakers waves.
beam side.
canvas sails.
whorl propeller.
endured suffered.

15

Hope had grown grey hairs,
　　Hope had mourning on,
Trenched with tears, carved with cares,
　　Hope was twelve hours gone;
And frightful a nightfall folded rueful a day
Nor rescue, only rocket and lightship, shone,
　　And lives at last were washing away:
To the shrouds they took, – they shook in the hurling and
　　　　　　　　　　　　　horrible airs.

35

40

mourning black clothes worn as a mark of respect for the dead.

folded unfolded.
rueful bitter, terrible.
rocket distress flares.

shrouds sails; sheets in which dead bodies are wrapped

16

One stirred from the rigging to save
The wild woman-kind below,
With a rope's end round the man, handy and brave —
He was pitched to his death at a blow,
For all his dreadnought breast and braids of thew: 45
They could not tell him for hours, dandled the to and fro
Through the cobbled foam-fleece. What could he do
With the burl of the fountains of air, buck and the flood of the
wave?

dreadnought mighty strength and courage.
braids of thew muscles.
dandled dangled like a child from his mother's arms.
cobbled hard, grey.
burl blow of the rising wave.
buck kicking like a horse.

17

They fought with God's cold —
And they could not and fell to the deck 50
(Crushed them) or water (and drowned them) or rolled
With the sea-romp over the wreck.
Night roared, with the heart-break hearing a heart-broke
rabble,
The woman's wailing, the crying of child without check —
Till a lioness arose breasting the babble, 55
A prophetess towered in the tumult, a virginal tongue told.

without check unceasing, unstoppable.

tumult noise.
told rang like a bell.

19

Sister, a sister calling
A master, her master and mine! —
And the inboard seas run swirling and hawling;
The rash smart sloggering brine 60
Blinds her; but she that weather sees one thing, one;
Has one fetch in her: she rears herself to divine
Ears, and the call of the tall nun
To the men in the tops and the tackle rode over the storm's
brawling.

inboard seas the ship is awash.
hawling dragging down.
smart stinging.
sloggering overpowering.
brine salt water.
fetch supreme effort.
tops mast tops.
brawling noise, howling, fighting.

24

Away in the loveable west, 65
On a pastoral forehead of Wales,
I was under a roof here, I was at rest,
And they the prey of the gales;
She to the black-about air, to the breaker, the thickly
Falling flakes, to the throng that catches and quails 70
Was calling 'O Christ, Christ, come quickly';
The cross to her she calls Christ to her, christens her wild-worst
Best.

quails makes flinch.
christens her wild-worst Best calls her moment of supreme suffering her moment of greatest happiness.

☆

Thinking/Talking Points

▷ What impact does this extract make upon you?
Pick out two or three details you particularly liked.

▷ How do you picture Death (stanza 11)?
How do you imagine the movement of the 'sour scythe' and 'blear share' (line 8)?

▷ 'Hurling the haven behind,' (line 18)
See if you can describe this movement in your own words.

▷ What do you think is meant by:
'the widow-making unchilding unfathering deeps' (line 24)?

▷ How do you picture Hope (stanza 15)?

▷ Look at the episode of the sailor's death (stanza 16).
What makes the way Hopkins describes it so different from this account in *The Times* newspaper:
'One brave sailor, who was safe in the rigging, went down to try to save a child or woman who was drowning on deck. He was secured by a rope to the rigging, but a wave dashed him against the bulwarks, and when daylight dawned his headless body, detained by the rope, was seen swaying to and fro with the waves.'

▷ How do you picture the Sister (lines 55–63, 69–72)?

Read through the extract a few more times.
You will find it works best if you read it aloud.

Assignments

○ Prepare a performance of the extract for a group of voices. (This could be done on tape, perhaps using instruments as well.)

○ Using details from the whole of this unit and also adding lots of your own ideas, write an account of this shipwreck from the point of view of one of the survivors
either (a) on board
or   (b) in that nightmare voyage in the lifeboat.
Describe exactly what happened to you:
    How you felt as the ship sailed from Bremen.
    When you became aware that the ship was running into difficulties.
    What you saw, heard and felt as the ship struck the sandbank.
    The scenes on deck, the storm and the buck of the sea.
    The behaviour of your friends, fellow-passengers and the crew.
    What it was like climbing the rigging or clambering into the lifeboat.
    The experience of hanging on in the cold and wet for so long with no sign of rescue.
    How you were eventually saved.

Describe the way the experience changed the way you saw the sea and, perhaps, yourself.

Shakespeare
from RICHARD III

Have you ever got into trouble swimming?
Have you ever been thrown into a pond or a swimming pool?
Do you ever have nightmares about drowning?
Can you imagine what it would be like?

This extract comes from Shakespeare's play *Richard III*.
Clarence, a prisoner in the Tower of London, wakes up, relieved, from a terrible dream he has had and tells his gaoler about it. What Clarence does not realise, however, is that the dream was a warning. His wicked brother, Gloucester, has arranged to have Clarence murdered. Shortly after telling Brakenbury about his dream, Clarence is drowned in a huge cask of Malmsey wine.

Read through these lines a few times and then look at the questions that follow.

from Richard III

Methoughts that I had broken from the Tower	**methoughts** *I thought.*
And was embarked to cross to Burgundy,	**embarked** *on board ship.*
And in my company my brother Gloucester,	
Who from my cabin tempted me to walk	
Upon the hatches. Thence we looked toward England 5	**hatches** *the deck.*
And cited up a thousand heavy times,	**thence** *from there.*
During the wars of York and Lancaster,	**cited up** *recalled.*
That had befallen us. As we paced along	
Upon the giddy footing of the hatches,	**giddy footing of the**
Methought that Gloucester stumbled, and in falling 10	**hatches** *toing and froing deck which made us feel giddy.*
Struck me (that thought to stay him) overboard	**stay** *support.*
Into the tumbling billows of the main.	**billows** *waves.*
O Lord, methought what pain it was to drown!	**main** *ocean.*
What dreadful noise of water in mine ears!	
What sights of ugly death within mine eyes! 15	
Methoughts I saw a thousand fearful wracks;	**wracks** *shipwrecks.*
A thousand men that fishes gnawed upon;	
Wedges of gold, great anchors, heaps of pearl,	
Inestimable stones, unvalued jewels,	**inestimable** *too many to*
All scattered in the bottom of the sea. 20	*count.*
Some lay in dead men's skulls, and in the holes	**unvalued** *priceless.*
Where eyes did once inhabit there were crept,	
As 'twere in scorn of eyes, reflecting gems	
That wooed the slimy bottom of the deep	
And mocked the dead bones that lay scattered by. 25	

... often did I strive
To yield the ghost, but still the envious flood
Stopped in my soul and would not let it forth
To find the empty, vast, and wandering air,
But smothered it within my panting bulk,   30
Who almost burst to belch it in the sea.

[But then] my dream was lengthened after life.
O, then began the tempest to my soul!
I passed, methought, the melancholy flood,
With that sour ferryman which poets write of,   35
Unto the kingdom of perpetual night.
The first that there did greet my stranger soul
Was my great father-in-law, renowned Warwick,
Who spake aloud, 'What scourge for perjury
Can this dark monarchy afford false Clarence?'   40
And so he vanished. Then came wandering by
A shadow like an angel, with bright hair
Dabbled in blood, and he shrieked out aloud,
'Clarence is come, false, fleeting, perjured Clarence,
That stabbed me in the field by Tewkesbury.   45
Seize on him, Furies, take him unto torment!'
With that, methought, a legion of foul fiends
Environed me and howled in mine ears
Such hideous cries that with the very noise
I, trembling, waked, and for a season after   50
Could not believe but that I was in hell,
Such terrible impression made my dream.

Act I sc.iv

to yield the ghost to die.
envious flood spiteful sea.
stopped in held in (with a stopper).
bulk body.

tempest storm.
the melancholy flood the dismal river Styx in the underworld.
that sour ferryman Charon, the boatman who rowed the dead across the river Styx.
stranger newly arrived.
renowned famous.
scourge punishment.
perjury lying.
this dark monarchy Hell.
afford provide for.
false deceitful, disloyal.

fleeting fickle, unreliable.

Furies wild tormenting creatures who pursue the guilty.
fiends devils.
environed surrounded.

☆

Thinking/Talking Points

▷   Which details in the nightmare do you find most horrible?
    Which phrases make you *feel* as if you're drowning?

▷   What did the dream tell Clarence about his brother?

▷   What do you feel as you read this:
    'Some [jewels] lay in dead men's skulls, and in the holes
    Where eyes did once inhabit there were crept,
    As 'twere in scorn of eyes, reflecting gems
    That wooed the slimy bottom of the deep
    And mocked the dead bones that lay scattered by.'
    (a)   Think about how eyes and jewels are like/unlike one another.
    (b)   Think about the effect of putting the phrases 'reflecting gems' and 'slimy
          bottom of the deep' side by side.
    (c)   What do you think the speaker means when he says the jewels *mocked* the
          dead bones?

▷ Look again at lines 37–41.
How do you feel as you read this passage?
Which details produce those feelings?

▷ Where does Clarence find himself after death?
What makes that place terrifying?
How do *you* imagine that place?

▷ Do you think Clarence believes he deserves to suffer as he did in his dream?
Does that make the suffering worse?

Read through the extract again a few times.
Are there interesting details you hadn't noticed before?

Assignments

○ *The Worst Thing in the World*
What is your worst nightmare? Is there a terrifying situation in which you
often find yourself in dreams or fantasies?
See if you can describe it so vividly that the reader can share the terror.

○ *As Time Stood Still*
Concentrating upon a very short period of time, see if you can write an account
of a violent death as the subject might experience it (e.g. in a fire; in a climbing
accident; in an accident at a fair; in a plunging aeroplane).

○ *Richard III* was one of Shakespeare's earliest successes. Twenty years after he
wrote it, in his last play, he wrote this song about a drowned king. Compare it
with the lines we looked at in detail and explain why its impact is so different:

> Full fathom five thy father lies;
>   Of his bones are coral made;
> Those are pearls that were his eyes;
>   Nothing of him that doth fade,
> But doth suffer a sea-change
> Into something rich and strange.
> Sea-nymphs hourly ring his knell.

> from *The Tempest* Act I sc.ii

Some further reading

Compare Clarence's nightmare with the opening of Golding's novel
Pincher Martin.
A. Bierce   Short story: *An Occurrence at Owl Creek Bridge*

★

Shelley
OZYMANDIAS

Who do you think was the greatest King or Queen of all time?
What do you know about that ruler's life and personality?
How do you think such a monarch would get on in today's world?

What sort of person does the phrase 'king of kings' make you imagine?
What qualities do you think The Ruler of the World would need?

Read through this sonnet a few times before thinking about the points which
follow.

Ozymandias

I met a traveller from an antique land
Who said: Two vast and trunkless legs of stone
Stand in the desert . . . Near them, on the sand,
Half sunk, a shattered visage lies, whose frown,
And wrinkled lip, and sneer of cold command,   5
Tell that its sculptor well those passions read
Which yet survive, stamped on these lifeless things,
The hand that mocked them, and the heart that fed;
And on the pedestal these words appear:
'My name is Ozymandias, king of kings: 10
Look on my works, ye Mighty, and despair!'
Nothing beside remains. Round the decay
Of that colossal wreck, boundless and bare
The lone and level sands stretch far away.

sonnet *a poem of fourteen lines.*
trunkless *the rest of the body is missing.*
shattered *smashed to pieces.*
visage *face.*
sneer *sour, scornful expression.*
yet survive *still exist.*
stamped *recorded.*
pedestal *the base of the statue.*

despair *give up all hope.*

colossal *giant-like, huge.*
boundless *endless.*

Thinking/Talking Points

▷   What do you suppose is meant by 'an antique land'?
    What pictures do those words suggest to you?

▷   Why do you think the poet decided to invent 'the traveller' rather than tell us
    about this experience as if it had been his own?

▷   Read lines 4 and 5 again.
    What sort of face do you see?

▷   What do you think the poet means by '*cold* command'?
    How do you imagine Ozymandias talking?

▷ What sort of king do you imagine Ozymandias to have been? (e.g. How would he dress? Sit? Walk about his palace? How do you think he would treat his family? His servants? What would be his attitude to other kings? Is the phrase 'king of kings' familiar to you from anywhere else? Can you think of a modern ruler like Ozymandias?)

▷ Why do you think Ozymandias ordered the statue to be made?
What do you imagine it looked like when it was brand new?

▷ How do you think the sculptor felt when he received Ozymandias's command to create the statue?
How do you suppose Ozymandias treated him?

▷ Who do you think really had more power, the king or the sculptor? Why?

▷ Look again at the last five lines of the poem.
What do you think Ozymandias's words meant when they were sculpted?
Do you think they mean something different now?

Read through the sonnet again a few times and then choose your assignment.

Assignments

○ On your own or in a small group, make a giant picture or model of the statue of Ozymandias.

○ *The Commission*
Imagine you are the sculptor, Ezra, living in the Kingdom of Ozymandias. (Invent your own names for people and for places.)
Write an account of the day you were summoned to the King's palace and given instructions for the monument.
Describe first your workshop, then the messenger and then your journey to the palace. What sights did you see? What were your feelings?
Next, describe the palace itself, the ceremony, the behaviour of the courtiers, the atmosphere as you waited to be admitted to the throne-room.
Then tell us about Ozymandias himself. What were your first impressions? What did he look like? How did he talk to you? How did you feel about the commission? Were you feeling honoured or nervous?
Describe a session when you made your sketches of the King.
Describe the construction of the mighty statue: the technical problems and the way the workmen behaved.
Finally, describe the day on which Ozymandias came to view the finished piece. Were you pleased with your work? Was he?

○ Imagine you are Professor Eisenstein, the archaeologist who discovered the magnificent ruins of Ozymandias's palace.
In an article for a magazine, a talk or television documentary, describe the moment of discovery: your feelings and hopes.
What did your months of excavation unearth?
What did you learn about life under Ozymandias?
Make some drawings of the most interesting treasures.
You may like to make a plan of the palace itself.
What do your discoveries make you feel about Kings and Fame and Power?

Coleridge
KUBLA KHAN

Imagine a wild landscape.
What do you see? Huge jagged rocks, gaunt trees? An endless, waterless
desert? Sharp granite cliffs jutting over a raging sea? A sky the colour of blood?
A sickly moon? Hot, roaring wind or driving blizzard? Huge black birds
circling . . .? What do your ears and nostrils pick up?

Assignment 1

Describe a savage and remote place.
Describe how you might feel if you found yourself there.

The idea for this poem came to Coleridge in a dream.

Kubla Khan

In Xanadu did Kubla Khan
   A stately pleasure-dome decree:
Where Alph, the sacred river, ran
Through caverns measureless to man
   Down to a sunless sea,   5
So twice five miles of fertile ground
With walls and towers were girdled round;
And here were gardens bright with sinuous rills,
Where blossomed many an incense-bearing tree;
And here were forests ancient as the hills,   10
Enfolding sunny spots of greenery.

But Oh! that deep romantic chasm which slanted
Down the green hill athwart a cedarn cover!
A savage place! as holy and enchanted
As e'er beneath a waning moon was haunted   15
By woman wailing for her demon-lover!
And from this chasm, with ceaseless turmoil seething,
As if this Earth in fast thick pants were breathing,
A mighty fountain momently was forced:
Amid whose swift half-intermitted burst   20
Huge fragments vaulted like rebounding hail,
Or chaffy grain beneath the thresher's flail:
And 'mid these dancing rocks at once and ever
It flung up momently the sacred river.

decree order to be built.

measureless impossible to measure.

girdled round surrounded by.
sinuous rills winding streams.
incense heavy perfume.

chasm yawning gap.
athwart from side to side of.
cedarn cover shelter of cedar trees.
waning diminishing.
ceaseless unending.
turmoil commotion, confusion.
seething foaming furiously.
half-intermitted half checked, interrupted.
vaulted leapt up.
rebounding bouncing.
chaffy grain corn full of husks.
thresher's flail tool like a club used in harvesting to separate grain from chaff.

Five miles meandering with a mazy motion 25 **meandering** *winding this way and that.*
Through wood and dale the sacred river ran,   **mazy** *as if through a maze.*
Then reached the caverns measureless to man,
And sank in tumult to a lifeless ocean:
And 'mid this tumult Kubla heard from far   **tumult** *din.*
Ancestral voices prophesying war!   30 **prophesying** *predicting.*

    The shadow of the dome of pleasure
    Floated midway on the waves;
    Where was heard the mingled measure   **mingled measure** *blended harmonies, music.*
    From the fountain and the caves.
It was a miracle of rare device,   35 **of rare device** *cunningly made.*
A sunny pleasure-dome with caves of ice!

    A damsel with a dulcimer   **damsel** *young girl.*
    In a vision once I saw: **dulcimer** *a musical instrument rather like a zither.*
    It was an Abyssinian maid,
    And on her dulcimer she played,   40
    Singing of Mount Abora.   **Mount Abora** *believed by some to be Paradise.*
    Could I revive within me
    Her symphony and song,
    To such a deep delight 'twould win me
That with music loud and long,   45
I would build that dome in air,
That sunny dome! those caves of ice!
And all who heard should see them there,
And all should cry, Beware! Beware!
His flashing eyes, his floating hair!   50
Weave a circle round him thrice,   **weave a circle** *a magic ritual to protect the inspired poet from interruptions.*
And close your eyes with holy dread,
For he on honey-dew hath fed,
And drunk the milk of Paradise.

Thinking/Talking Points

▷ What was the effect on you of hearing the poem?

▷ Picture Kubla Khan.
How tall is he? Of what complexion? What is he wearing?

▷ Imagine the pleasure-dome.
What is it built of? What sounds, what smells come from it?
What sorts of things do you imagine Kubla Khan collecting inside?

▷ What pictures does the phrase 'Through caverns measureless to man' make you see?
Think what it would be like to sail on 'a sunless sea'.

▷ How do you imagine the movement, the noises of the river?
What are the shapes, the textures of the rocks?
What colours would you use to paint the scene?

▷ What is special about the trees in the garden (line 9)?

▷ What do you think the difference is between a 'holy' and an 'enchanted' place? (line 14)
Savage . . . holy . . . enchanted . . . haunted . . .
In your own words, describe the mixture of feelings which the place gives you.

▷ How do you imagine a 'demon-lover'?

▷ Look again at lines 17–24. Read them aloud.
(a)   Which words describe movement?
(b)   Describe in your own words what the passage makes you see.

▷ How is the impression of the pleasure-dome in lines 31–36 different from that created in lines 6–11?

▷ How do you picture the Abyssinian maid?

▷ Which details in the poem are most like the experience of dreams?

Read through the poem again a few times. Have you ever read anything like this before or seen pictures or heard music which created a similar mood?

Assignments

○ In pairs or a small group, prepare a performance of this poem. Think about the various ways you could use voices to create different effects to match the changing mood of the poem. You may wish to use musical instruments or recorded music to accompany your reading.
Alternatively, you could see if you could produce a mime or dance inspired by the poem.

○ Write about a boat journey down the sacred river Alph.
Add plenty of your own ideas to those we're given in the poem.
You may write in verse or prose.

○ *My Pleasure-dome*
What would your own pleasure-dome contain?
Think about the building, the gardens, the atmosphere.
Where would you build it? Who would be allowed in?
Choose a suitable name for it.
You may like to produce an elaborate map or diagram of the place.

○ The lines we have of *Kubla Khan* are the incomplete memory of a trance-dream which Coleridge had under the influence of opium. He believed that he dreamed two or three hundred lines of verse. When he woke up, he began to write them down, but he was interrupted by a visitor.
How do you think the poem could have continued? With an account of those prophesied wars? With a further change of the pleasure-dome? With a flight over the rest of Kubla Khan's kingdom?
See if you can write a few dozen lines which seem to grow
either (a) from where the poem ends now
or (b) from some earlier point in the poem.

★

THE JEWEL STAIRS' GRIEVANCE
and
THE RIVER-MERCHANT'S WIFE:
A LETTER

Look carefully at this poem and at the translator's note.

The Jewel Stairs' Grievance

The jewelled steps are already quite white with dew,
It is so late that the dew soaks my gauze stockings,
And I let down the crystal curtain
And watch the moon through the clear autumn.

*Note: Jewel stairs, therefore a palace. Grievance, therefore there is something to
complain of. Gauze stockings, therefore a court lady, not a servant who complains.
Clear autumn, therefore he has no excuse on account of weather. Also she has come
early, for the dew has not merely whitened the stairs, but has soaked her stockings.
The poem is especially prized because she utters no direct reproach.*

Now read through this poem a few times before thinking about the points
which follow.

The River-Merchant's Wife: a Letter

While my hair was still cut straight across my forehead
I played about the front gate, pulling flowers.
You came by on bamboo stilts, playing horse,
You walked about my seat, playing with blue plums.
And we went on living in the village of Chōkan: *5*
Two small people, without dislike or suspicion.

At fourteen I married My Lord you.
I never laughed, being bashful.
Lowering my head, I looked at the wall.
Called to, a thousand times, I never looked back.   *10*

At fifteen I stopped scowling,
I desired my dust to be mingled with yours
Forever and forever and forever.
Why should I climb the look out?

At sixteen you departed,   *15*
You went into far Ku-tō-en, by the river of swirling eddies,
And you have been gone five months.
The monkeys make sorrowful noise overhead.

You dragged your feet when you went out.
By the gate now, the moss is grown, the different mosses,   *20*
Too deep to clear them away!
The leaves fall early this autumn, in wind,
The paired butterflies are already yellow with August
Over the grass in the West garden;
They hurt me. I grow older.   *25*
If you are coming down through the narrows of the river Kiang,
Please let me know beforehand,
And I will come out to meet you
    As far as Chō-fù-Sa.

Thinking/Talking Points

▷ In what way(s) do you think this poem is similar to *The Jewel Stairs' Grievance*?

▷ What does the poem tell us about the ages of the merchant and his wife?

▷ What was the girl's attitude to getting married?
How did it change?
How are we told about her feelings?

▷ Notice how many descriptive details there are in stanza 4.
What effect does each of those details have upon you?

▷ Look again at stanza 5.
Which details tell us about the speaker's mood?

▷ Did you like the way the poem was written?

Read through the poem again a few times.

Assignments

○ Draw a picture to illustrate one of the poems.

○ Write the River-Merchant's reply.

○ See if you can write a poem in a similar style on one of the following themes.
Use very few descriptive details and try to suggest the speaker's attitude rather
than saying directly how he/she feels.
    The feelings of a son at his mother's graveside
    Thoughts of a young mother about her baby
    The feelings of a horseman as the winter sun sets
    An observer's thoughts as he watches a huge army march towards the
    battlefield
    A girl awaiting her boyfriend's visit

Some further reading

Ezra Pound   *The Return*
James Joyce   *On the Beach at Fontana*

Upstream from Camelot lies a silent island on which stands a grey castle. Inside the castle is a Lady who spends her days weaving. Sometimes she sings.

The Lady has been told that she may not look from her window towards Camelot and so she watches what happens outside reflected in a mirror on the wall of her room. She sees people going to and from Camelot. She weaves some of what she sees in the mirror into her work.

One day, Sir Lancelot passes by. Hearing him sing, the Lady rises from her work and looks directly through the window at the knight. Immediately, her work is whirled away and the mirror cracks.

The Lady descends from the castle to the river and finds a boat. She lies down in it and casts herself adrift on the tide. Singing her swan-song, the Lady drifts in the boat towards Camelot. As she reaches the outskirts, she dies. The inhabitants, including Lancelot, come to view the body.

Have you ever come across a story like this before?
Why do you think so many people enjoy fables, folk-tales, fairy tales and fantasy literature?
Can you think of any popular novels, films or television programmes set in imaginary and mysterious places? What things make the stories 'unreal'?

Do you ever daydream in ways more like fantasy than real life?
What sorts of people and places do you picture?
Do you find certain situations haunt your imagination?

What pictures do the words 'Camelot' and 'Sir Lancelot' suggest to you?
How do you imagine the Lady in this story? And her castle?
What sort of landscape do you see?

If you were asked to write a version of this story for primary school children, which bits would you expand, colour or change? (e.g. Would you tell your readers more about the characters of Lancelot and the Lady? What descriptive details would you add to bring the story to life? Would you try to 'explain' why any of this happens?)

If the story were made into a song, what kind of song would it be?
What sort of music do you think would be appropriate?

Here is Tennyson's version of the story. Read it through a couple of times and then consider the points which follow.

The Lady of Shalott

Part I

On either side the river lie
Long fields of barley and of rye,
That clothe the wold and meet the sky;
And thro' the field the road runs by

    To many-tower'd Camelot;   5

And up and down the people go,
Gazing where the lilies blow
Round an island there below,

    The island of Shalott.

Willows whiten, aspens quiver,   10
Little breezes dusk and shiver
Thro' the wave that runs for ever
By the island in the river

    Flowing down to Camelot.

Four gray walls, and four gray towers,   15
Overlook a space of flowers,
And the silent isle imbowers

    The Lady of Shalott.

By the margin, willow-veil'd,
Slide the heavy barges trail'd   20
By slow horses; and unhail'd
The shallop flitteth silken-sail'd

    Skimming down to Camelot:

But who hath seen her wave her hand?
Or at the casement seen her stand?   25
Or is she known in all the land,

    The Lady of Shalott?

Only reapers, reaping early
In among the bearded barley,
Hear a song that echoes cheerly   30
From the river winding clearly,

    Down to tower'd Camelot:

And by the moon the reaper weary,
Piling sheaves in uplands airy,
Listening, whispers ''Tis the fairy   35

    Lady of Shalott.'

wold *open, hilly countryside.*

blow *bloom.*

aspen *a tree whose leaves tremble in a breeze.*

imbowers *is home for.*

shallop *a light, open boat.*
flitteth *glides swiftly.*

reapers *corn gatherers.*

Part II

There she weaves by night and day
A magic web with colours gay,
She has heard a whisper say,
A curse is on her if she stay   *40*
    To look down to Camelot.
She knows not what the curse may be,
And so she weaveth steadily,
And little other care hath she,
    The Lady of Shalott.   *45*

And moving thro' a mirror clear
That hangs before her all the year,
Shadows of the world appear.
There she sees the highway near
    Winding down to Camelot: *50*
There the river eddy whirls,
And there the surly village-churls,
And the red cloaks of market girls,
    Pass onward from Shalott.

eddy *small whirpool.*

surly *rough, sullen.*
churls *working men.*

Sometimes a troop of damsels glad,   *55*
An abbot on an ambling pad,
Sometimes a curly shepherd-lad,
Or long-haired page in crimson clad,
    Goes by to tower'd Camelot;
And sometimes thro' the mirror blue   *60*
The knights come riding two and two:
She hath no loyal knight and true,
    The Lady of Shalott.

damsels *young girls.*

ambling pad *a horse,*
walking at a leisurely pace.

But in her web she still delights
To weave the mirror's magic sights,   *65*
For often through the silent nights
A funeral, with plumes and lights,
    And music, went to Camelot:
Or when the moon was overhead,
Came two young lovers lately wed;   *70*
'I am half sick of shadows,' said
    The Lady of Shalott.

Part III

A bow-shot from her bower-eaves,
He rode between the barley-sheaves,
The sun came dazzling through the leaves,   *75*
And flamed upon the brazen greaves
    Of bold Sir Lancelot.
A red-cross knight for ever kneel'd
To a lady in his shield,
That sparkled on the yellow field,   *80*
    Beside remote Shalott.

The gemmy bridle glitter'd free,
Like to some branch of stars we see
Hung in the golden Galaxy.
The bridle bells rang merrily   *85*
    As he rode down to Camelot:
And from his blazon'd baldric slung
A mighty silver bugle hung,
And as he rode his armour rung,
    Beside remote Shalott.   *90*

All in the blue unclouded weather
Thick-jewell'd shone the saddle-leather,
The helmet and the helmet-feather
Burn'd like one burning flame together,
    As he rode down to Camelot.   *95*
As often thro' the purple night,
Below the starry clusters bright,
Some bearded meteor, trailing light,
    Moves over still Shalott,

His broad clear brow in sunlight glow'd;   *100*
On burnish'd hooves his war-horse trode;
From underneath his helmet flow'd
His coal-black curls as on he rode,
    As he rode down to Camelot.
From the bank and from the river   *105*
He flash'd into the crystal mirror,
'Tirra lirra,' by the river
    Sang Sir Lancelot.

She left the web, she left the loom,
She made three paces thro' the room,   *110*
She saw the water-lily bloom,
She saw the helmet and the plume,
    She look'd down to Camelot.
Out flew the web and floated wide;
The mirror crack'd from side to side;   *115*
'The curse is come upon me!' cried
    The Lady of Shalott.

bower-eaves *the sloping roof of her bedroom.*

brazen greaves *brass-coloured armour.*

gemmy *jewelled.*

blazon'd baldric *a belt hanging from the shoulder, decorated with the knight's coat-of-arms.*

burnish'd *polished.*

Part IV

In the stormy east-wind straining,
The pale yellow woods were waning,
The broad stream in his banks complaining,   120
Heavily the low sky raining
    Over tower'd Camelot;
Down she came and found a boat
Beneath a willow left afloat,
And round about the prow she wrote   125
    The Lady of Shalott.

And down the river's dim expanse –
Like some bold seer in a trance,
Seeing all his own mischance –
With a glassy countenance   130
    Did she look to Camelot.
And at the closing of the day
She loosed the chain, and down she lay;
The broad stream bore her far away,
    The Lady of Shalott.   135

Lying, robed in snowy white
That loosely flew to left and right –
The leaves upon her falling light –
Thro' the noises of the night
    She floated down to Camelot: 140
And as the boat-head wound along
The willowy hills and fields among,
They heard her singing her last song,
    The Lady of Shalott.

Heard a carol, mournful, holy,   145
Chanted loudly, chanted lowly,
Till her blood was frozen slowly,
And her eyes were darken'd wholly,
    Turn'd to tower'd Camelot;
For ere she reached upon the tide   150
The first house by the water-side,
Singing in her song she died,
    The Lady of Shalott.

Under tower and balcony,
By garden-wall and gallery,   155
A gleaming shape she floated by,
Dead-pale between the houses high,
    Silent into Camelot.
Out upon the wharfs they came,
Knight and burgher, lord and dame,   160
And round her prow they read her name,
    The Lady of Shalott.

seer *one who knows the future.*

mournful *full of sadness.*

burgher *citizen.*

90

Who is this? and what is here?
And in the lighted palace near
Died the sound of royal cheer;   165   *cheer* merrymaking.
And they cross'd themselves for fear,
    All the knights at Camelot:
But Lancelot mused a little space;
He said, 'She has a lovely face;
God in His mercy lend her grace,   170
    The Lady of Shalott.'

☆

Thinking/Talking Points

▷   Was the poem what you expected?
Which descriptive details did you particularly like?
How would you describe the mood of Tennyson's poem?

▷   What were the biggest differences between Tennyson's version and the outline
you read at the beginning?
Do you think the summary missed out important details?

▷   'On either side of the river there are long fields of barley and rye. A road runs
through them to Camelot with its many towers. Travellers gaze down from the
road to the island of Shalott while lilies grow.'
(a)   Is this a fair summary of the first stanza?
        If you think it isn't, improve it until you are satisfied with it.
(b)   What do you think has been lost by turning poetry into prose?
        See if you can explain why the prose version has a quite different feel
        about it from the poem.
(c)   In pairs, try repeating this exercise with another stanza.
        Make a careful paraphrase (prose version) and then see what is 'lost'.

▷   What do you notice about the shape of each stanza of the poem?
What is the effect of so many repetitions?

Read through the poem again a few times to see which details are most
effective. Are there any words or phrases you don't understand? What do you
like/dislike about the story and the way Tennyson tells it?

Assignment

This is an exercise for which a large dictionary and a thesaurus would be useful.

○ Choose one of the following outlines for a poem. Working singly or in pairs, see if you can write a piece in a style similar to Tennyson's.

Begin by deciding on the mood you wish to create.

Find as many words and phrases and images as you can which suggest that mood.

Think about the place where the events take place.

Collect words and phrases to describe it.

Think about the weather, the time of day, the season.

Decide on how the creatures/characters in the story will be described.

Think about whether it will be a good idea to have a regular rhyming pattern.

Will there be any phrases which are regularly repeated, as in Tennyson's poem?

Will you vary the lengths of lines as Tennyson does?

(a) A swan floats down a river. It is dying and singing its farewell. At first the song is as dismal as its surroundings but gradually it swells into a song of rejoicing.

(b) A girl is seduced by a handsome but wicked man. She dies, shamed, and her sister vows revenge. Eventually she manages to seduce the Earl and, when he is asleep, she stabs him, wraps his body in a sheet and presents it to his mother.

(c) Thorn-Rose (Sleeping Beauty) lies asleep. One day a young Prince breaks through the brambles which surround her and wakes her with a kiss.

(d) Mariana, jilted by her fiancé, lives in an old and remote country house, pining for her lover whom she always hopes will come but who never does.

You may like to illustrate your poem.

★

LA BELLE DAME SANS MERCI

In this poem, a knight tells of his seduction by a supernatural beauty.

La Belle Dame sans Merci

A ballad

'O what can ail thee, Knight-at-arms,
Alone and palely loitering?
The sedge has wither'd from the lake,
And no birds sing.

'O what can ail thee, Knight-at-arms,   5
So haggard and so woe-begone?
The squirrel's granary is full,
And the harvest's done.

'I see a lily on thy brow,
With anguish moist and fever dew,   10
And on thy cheeks a fading rose
Fast withereth too.'

'I met a lady in the meads,
Full beautiful – a faery's child,
Her hair was long, her foot was light,   15
And her eyes were wild.

'I made a garland for her head,
And bracelets too, and fragrant zone;
She look'd at me as she did love,
And made sweet moan.   20

'I set her on my pacing steed,
And nothing else saw all day long,
For sidelong would she bend and sing
A faery's song.

'She found me roots of relish sweet,   25
And honey wild and manna dew,
And sure in language strange she said
"I love thee true."

La Belle Dame sans Merci
*The Lovely Lady Who Has
No Pity.*

ail *distress, sadden.*
loitering *hanging about
the place idly.*
sedge *a kind of grass which
grows near water.*

**haggard and . . .woe-
begone** *wild-looking, care-
worn, dejected, sad.*
granary *store-house.*

anguish *distress, torment.*

meads *meadows.*

garland *a crown of flowers
or leaves.*
fragrant zone *a girdle or
belt of sweetly smelling
flowers.*
made sweet moan *spoke
lovingly.*
steed *horse.*

relish *taste.*
manna dew *a magical,
refreshing drink.*

'She took me to her elfin grot,   **grot** *cave.*
And there she wept and sigh'd full sore;   *30*
And there I shut her wild wild eyes
With kisses four.

'And there she lulled me asleep
And there I dream'd – Ah! woe betide!
The latest dream I ever dream'd   *35*   **latest** *last.*
On the cold hill's side.

'I saw pale kings and princes too,
Pale warriors, death-pale were they all:
Who cried – "La belle Dame sans merci
Hath thee in thrall!"   *40*   **in thrall** *captive, like a*
                                                                         slave.
                                                                         gloam *dusk, twilight.*
'I saw their starv'd lips in the gloam
With horrid warning gaped wide
And I awoke and found me here
On the cold hill's side.

'And this is why I sojourn here   *45*   **sojourn** *pause, rest.*
Alone and palely loitering,
Though the sedge is wither'd from the lake,
And no birds sing.'

Thinking/Talking Points

▷ How would you describe the mood, the atmosphere of the poem?

▷ Why do you think we are given no clues about where or when this episode takes place?

▷ Why do you think the poet writes the story as a conversation?

▷ How do you imagine the Knight?
Which details give you that impression?

▷ How do you picture the Lady?
Which words in the poem suggest that picture?

▷ Do you think the poem is best read silently or read aloud?

Read through the poem again a few times before choosing your assignment.

Assignments

○ *The Knight's Tale*
Use Keats's poem as a starting point for your own story.
Imagine you are the Knight.
Where had you been, where were you going?
Describe the landscape you were passing through and the weather.
What thoughts were passing through your head just before your encounter with La Belle Dame sans Merci?
Describe your meeting with the Lady.
Describe her appearance, her voice, her manner and how you felt in her presence. Did you have any doubts about her?
Describe your journey to the cave ('grot').
What was it like?
What were your feelings as you entered?
When and how did you realise the mistake you had made?

○ *The Mermaid's/Siren's/Femme-Fatale's/Proud Beauty's Ballad*
Using some details from Keats's poem but adding plenty of ideas of your own, tell the story, in verse or prose, of a hero's undoing, from his seducer's point of view.

○ Write a ballad in which a young girl tells of her seduction by a Don Juan/ Casanova/Lady's Man.

○ Produce some pictures for Keats's poem.

★

SPACEPOEM 3: OFF COURSE

If possible, work in pairs on the following poem.

Think about the title and then read through the poem a few times to see if you can decide at what point things start to go 'off course'.

How many stages do you think there are in the story?
Where do they begin and end?

Then see if you can work out how Edwin Morgan has made the poem.
Do words have the same meaning each time they are used?

Spacepoem 3: Off Course

the golden flood   the weightless seat
the cabin song   the pitch black
the growing beard   the floating crumb
the shining rendezvous   the orbit wisecrack
the hot spacesuit   the smuggled mouth-organ   5
the imaginary somersault   the visionary sunrise
the turning continents   the space debris
the golden lifeline   the space walk
the crawling deltas   the camera moon
the pitch velvet   the rough sleep   10
the crackling headphone   the space silence
the turning earth   the lifeline continents
the cabin sunrise   the hot flood
the shining spacesuit   the growing moon
   the crackling somersault   the smuggled orbit   15
   the rough moon   the visionary rendezvous
   the weightless headphone   the cabin debris
   the floating lifeline   the pitch sleep
   the crawling camera   the turning silence
   the space crumb   the crackling beard   20
   the orbit mouth-organ   the floating song

☆

Thinking/Talking Points

▷ Think about the phrase 'golden flood' at the beginning of the poem.
What impression of the launch does the phrase give you?
What pictures does it make you see?
Does the phrase have a different feel about it when we know what is going to happen later in the poem?

▷ What do you think the 'cabin song' might have been about?
What mood do you imagine the crew to be in?
What other phrase(s) tell us about their mood?

▷ How does the poet give us a sense of time passing?

▷ 'the smuggled mouth-organ'
Why do you think it needed to be 'smuggled'?
Why do you think it was smuggled?

▷ Pick out four words which appear in the poem more than once and see how the meaning and/or the mood they suggest changes.

▷ What does the last line of the poem suggest to you?

Read through the poem again a few times to see what else deserves attention. Are there any words or phrases you don't understand? Are there any interesting details you hadn't noticed before?

Assignments

○ *Spacepoem 3: The Revised Versions*
  (a) Collect the words which are used only once in the poem.
      Can you see any ways in which they could be combined to make any extra lines?
      Where would you put them?
  (b) See if you can produce a poem which uses each of *Spacepoem 3*'s words three times.
      Your poem should tell a story but it will be a different one from Edwin Morgan's.

○ *Poem 99* (or whatever)
Use this technique of making lots of different phrases from a handful of words to tell a story of your own.
It could be about anything – here are a few ideas:

The picnic	Boy meets girl
Camping expedition	Birthday party
Storm in three stages	Murder!

○ Prepare a performance of Edwin Morgan's poem for one, two or a group of voices.
Think about some suitable accompanying gestures and/or music and/or sound effects.

★

Morgan
THE FIRST MEN ON MERCURY

How do you think people would react if a spaceship landed in the middle of your town?
What would be your attitude to visitors from another planet?
Why might they have come?

Assignment 1

○ We suggest you work in pairs.
Take thirty minutes to prepare a performance of this poem.

The First Men on Mercury

– We come in peace from the third planet.
Would you take us to your leader?

– Bawr stretter! Bawr. Bawr. Stretterhawl?

– This is a little plastic model
of the solar system, with working parts.   *5*
You are here and we are there and we
are now here with you, is this clear?

– Gawl horrop. Bawr. Abawrhannahanna!

– Where we come from is blue and white
with brown, you see we call the brown   *10*
here 'land', the blue is 'sea', and the white
is 'clouds' over land and sea, we live
on the surface of the brown land,
all round is sea and clouds. We are 'men'.
Men come –   *15*

– Glawp men! Gawrbenner menko. Menhawl?

– Men come in peace from the third planet
which we call 'earth'. We are earthmen.
Take us earthmen to your leader.

100

– Thmen? Thmen? Bawr. Bawrhossop. 20
Yuleeda tan hanna. Harrabost yuleeda.

– I am the yuleeda. You see my hands,
we carry no benner, we come in peace.
The spaceways are all stretterhawn.

– Glawn peacemen all horrabhanna tantko! 25
Tan come at'mstrossop. Glawp yuleeda!

– Atoms are peacegawl in our harraban.
Menbat worrabost from tan hannahanna.

– You men we know bawrhossoptant. Bawr.
We know yuleeda. Go strawg backspetter quick. 30

– We cantantabawr, tantingko backspetter now!

– Banghapper now! Yes, third planet back.
Yuleeda will go back bluc, white, brown
nowhanna! There is no more talk.

– Gawl han fasthapper? 35
– No. You must go back to your planet.
Go back in peace, take what you have gained
but quickly.

– Stretterworra gawl, gawl . . .

– Of course, but nothing is ever the same, 40
now is it? You'll remember Mercury.

Thinking/Talking Points

▷ Jot down some words to describe the mood of the two speakers
  (a) at the beginning
  (b) at the end of the poem.

▷ How do the Mercurians feel about the human visitors?
  Why do you think they feel that way?

Assignment 2

○   On your own or in small groups, produce a book of *Handy Mercurian Phrases for the Traveller*.
    Begin by trying to work out the meanings of some of the Mercurian words in the poem. Then invent some phrases likely to be useful in various situations, e.g. on the beach; at the hotel; shopping; on the Mercurian metro; eating out; meeting members of the Mercurian royal family . . .
    You may like to illustrate the book.

○   Write a not-too-serious *Mercurian's Guide to Britain*.
    Include the usual traveller's information:
    geography, flora and fauna of the place; brief history; present importance; famous people past and present; interesting places; local customs; transport; useful phrases for the visitor; laws you need to know . . .
    Remember your readers will not know about many things we take for granted so you will have some explaining to do, e.g. why the British enjoy queueing; the correct way to behave at football matches; the uses of the umbrella; the origin of 'punk'.

○   Imagine you are a Mercurian visitor to your town.
    Write a series of letters home about the extraordinary things you see and hear. Describe how you are treated by the earthlings and what you feel about their way of life.

○   You are appointed first Governor of the Earthlings' Colony of Mercury.
    Write an account of your experiences.

Some further reading

Jonathan Swift   *Voyage to Lilliput*
H.G. Wells   *First Men in the Moon*
                                        The Country of the Blind
                                        The Time Machine
Una Woodruff   *Amarant, the Flora and Fauna of Atlantis*
Alberto Manguel and Gianni Guadalupi   *The Dictionary of Imaginary Places*

★

BOMBARDMENT

Owen
THE SENTRY

Binyon
from FETCHING THE WOUNDED

What does the phrase 'The Great War' mean to you?
What pictures, what attitudes do you associate with the Somme,
Passchendaele, the Western Front?

The following poems were all written during the First World War. Read them
through a few times before considering the points which follow.

Bombardment

Four days the earth was rent and torn	*rent* wrenched apart.
By bursting steel,	
The houses fell about us;	
Three nights we dared not sleep,	
Sweating, and listening for the imminent crash 5	*imminent* threatened, expected at any time.
Which meant our death.	
The fourth night every man,	
Nerve-tortured, racked to exhaustion,	*racked* strained.
Slept, muttering and twitching,	
While the shells crashed overhead. 10	
The fifth day there came a hush;	
We left our holes	
And looked above the wreckage of the earth	
To where the white clouds moved in silent lines	
Across the untroubled blue. 15	

Thinking/Talking Points

Bombardment

▷ Write down as many words as you can to describe the state of mind of the men
(a) during (b) after the bombardment.

▷ What picture of the men does the phrase 'We left our holes' suggest to you?

▷ What is the effect of the final two lines of the poem on you?

The Sentry

We'd found an old Boche dug-out, and he knew,
And gave us hell, for shell on frantic shell
Hammered on top, but never quite burst through.
Rain, guttering down in waterfalls of slime,
Kept slush waist-high and rising hour by hour,   5
And choked the steps too thick with clay to climb.
What murk of air remained stank old, and sour
With fumes of whizz-bangs, and the smell of men
Who'd lived there years, and left their curse in the den,
If not their corpses . . .   10
      There we herded from the blast
Of whizz-bangs, but one found our door at last, –
Buffeting eyes and breath, snuffing the candles,
And thud! flump! thud! down the steep steps came thumping
And sploshing in the flood, deluging muck –   15
The sentry's body; then, his rifle, handles
Of old Boche bombs, and mud in ruck on ruck.
We dredged him up, for killed, until he whined
'O sir, my eyes – I'm blind – I'm blind, I'm blind!'
Coaxing, I held a flame against his lids   20
And said if he could see the least blurred light
He was not blind; in time he'd get all right.
'I can't,' he sobbed. Eyeballs, huge-bulged like squids',
Watch my dreams still; but I forgot him there
In posting Next for duty, and sending a scout   25
To beg a stretcher somewhere, and flound'ring about
To other posts under the shrieking air.

     * * *

Those other wretches, how they bled and spewed,
And one who would have drowned himself for good, –
I try not to remember these things now.   30
Let dread hark back for one word only: how
Half listening to that sentry's moans and jumps,
And the wild chattering of his broken teeth,
Renewed most horribly whenever crumps
Pummelled the roof and slogged the air beneath –   35
Through the dense din, I say, we heard him shout
'I see your lights!' But ours had long died out.

Boche German.
dug-out underground shelter against shells.

murk gloom, grubbiness.
whizz-bangs a type of shell.

buffeting bashing, thumping.
snuffing extinguishing.

deluging in a great rush, swamping.

ruck on ruck thick layer upon layer.

coaxing encouraging, reassuring.

squids sea creatures.

posting Next for duty setting the next man on watch.

crumps heavy explosive shells.
pummelled hammered-on.

Thinking/Talking Points

The Sentry

▷ Which descriptive details in the first stanza set the scene most vividly for you?

▷ Why do you think the soldiers call the shells 'whizz-bangs'?
What do you think their attitude to death is?

▷ What do you notice about the way the falling of the body is described?

▷ Why do you think the speaker was so apparently off-hand with the injured man?
Which detail reveals that the sentry's fate upset the speaker?

▷ What did you feel as you read the final stanza?

☆

from Fetching the Wounded

A sudden-call!
We leap to ground, and I forget it all.
Each hurries on his errand; lanterns swing;
Dark shapes cross and re-cross the rails; we bring
Stretchers, and pile and number them; and heap   *5*
The blankets ready, then we wait and keep
A listening ear. Nothing comes yet; all's still.
Only soft gusts upon the wires blow shrill
Fitfully, with a gentle spot of rain.
Then, ere one knows it, the long gradual train   *10*
Creeps quietly in and slowly stops. No sound
But a few voices' interchange. Around
Is the immense night-stillness, the expanse
Of faint stars over all the wounds of France.

Now stale odour of blood mingles with keen   *15*
Pure smell of grass and dew. Now lantern-sheen   *lantern-sheen* the light
Falls on brown faces opening patient eyes   *from their lanterns.*
And lips of gentle answers, where each lies
Supine upon his stretcher, black of beard   *supine* inert, lifelessly lying
Or with young cheeks; on caps and tunics smeared   *20* *on their backs.*
And stained, white bandages round foot or head
Or arm, discoloured here and there with red.
Sons of all corners of wide France; from Lille,
Douay, the land beneath the invader's heel,
Champagne, Touraine, the fisher-villages   *25*
Of Brittany, the valleyed Pyrenees,
Blue coasts of the South, old Paris streets. Argonne
Of ever smouldering battle, that anon
Leaps furious, brothered them in arms. They fell
In the trenched forest scarred with reeking shell.   *30*   *reeking* stinking.

106

Now strange the sound comes round them in the night
Of English voices. By the wavering light
Quickly we have borne them, one by one, to the air,
And sweating in the dark lift up with care,
Tense-sinewed, each to his place. The cars at last   *35*
Complete their burden: slowly, and then fast
We glide away.

Thinking/Talking Points

from *Fetching the Wounded*

▷ How would you describe the mood of the opening of this extract (lines 1–14)?
   Which details help to create that mood?

▷ What changes the mood in line 15?

▷ Which details give you the strongest impression of the wounded soldiers?

▷ How would you describe the mood of this extract as a whole?
   How do you think the speaker feels about the experiences he describes?

Read through the three poems again a few times to see what else deserves
attention. Are there any words or phrases you don't understand? Any
interesting details you hadn't noticed before?

Assignments

○ Here is an extract from a letter home written by a soldier. See if you can adapt
   some of the details into a poem in the style of one of those you have studied.

   'The sensations of going over the top are about as exhilarating as those dreams of
   falling over a precipice, when you see the rocks at the bottom surging up to you. I
   woke up without being squashed. Some didn't. There was an extraordinary
   exultation in the act of slowly walking forward, showing ourselves openly. There
   was no bugle and no drum, for which I was very sorry. I kept up a kind of chanting
   sing-song:
   Keep the Line straight!
   Not so fast on the left!
   Steady on the left!
      Not so fast!
   Then we were caught in a tornado of shells. The various "waves" were all broken up,
   and we carried on like a crowd moving off a cricket-field. When I looked back and
   saw the ground all crawling and wormy with wounded bodies, I felt no horror at all,
   but only an immense exultation at having got through the barrage. We were more
   than an hour moving over the open, and by the time we came to the German trench
   every Boche had fled. But a party of them had remained, lying low in a wood close
   behind us, and they gave us a very bad time for the next four hours. When we were
   marching along a sunken road, we got the wind up once. We knew we must have
   passed the German out-posts somewhere on our left rear. All at once the cry rang
   down, "Line the bank". There was a tremendous scurry of fixing bayonets, tugging of

breech-covers, and opening pouches, but when we peeped over, behold a solitary German, haring along towards us, with his head down and his arms stretched in front of him, as if he were going to take a high dive through the earth (which I have no doubt he would like to have done). Nobody offered to shoot him, he looked too funny; and that was our only prisoner that day!'

Wilfred Owen, 14th May 1917
(from *The Collected Poems of Wilfred Owen*, ed. C. Day Lewis, Chatto and Windus)

o Use the extract from the letter and/or details from the poems you have looked at as the basis of a short story. You may like to write it from the point of view of a German soldier.

o Essay: 'Many years later, these poems are still shocking and moving because the picture they paint of human suffering and of human care is as important to us now as it was to the poets.'
Do you agree? To what extent has any of the poems made you think more seriously about war or suffering? (Refer to particular details in the poems which impressed you in some way.)

o Produce some illustrations to accompany the poems.
Think carefully about the mood and tone of each poem and try to capture that in your picture.

Some further reading

Erich Remarque   *All Quiet on the Western Front*
I.M. Parsons   *Men Who March Away: Poems of the First World War, an anthology*
M. Middlebrook   *The Diaries of Pte. Horace Bruckshaw, Royal Marine Light Infantry, 1915–1916* (Scolar Press)
M. Hussey (ed.)   *Poetry of the First World War*
C. Day Lewis (ed.) *The Collected Poems of Wilfred Owen*
Robert Graves   *Goodbye to all that* (autobiography)
John Ellis   *Eye-Deep in Hell: The Western Front 1914–18*

★

Brecht

CHILDREN'S CRUSADE 1939

Here is a story from the Second World War.

In 'thirty nine, in Poland
a bloody battle took place,
turning many a town and village
into a wilderness.

The sister lost her brother,   5
the wife her husband in war,
the child between fire and rubble
could find his parents no more.

From Poland no news was forthcoming
neither letter nor printed word,   10
but in all the Eastern countries
a curious tale can be heard.

Snow fell when they told one another
this tale in an Eastern town
of a children's crusade that started   15
in Poland, in 'thirty-nine.

Along the highroads in squadrons   **squadron** *organised group.*
these hungry children tripped,
and on their way picked up others
in villages gutted and stripped.   20

They wanted to flee from the fighting
so that the nightmare would cease
and one day at last they'd arrive in
a country where there was peace.

They had a little leader   25
who was their prop and stay.   **prop and stay** *support,*
This leader had one great worry: *someone to rely on.*
he did not know the way.

A girl of eleven carried
a toddler of four without cease,   30
lacking nothing that makes a mother
but a country where there was peace.

A little Jewish boy marched in the troop,
with velvet collar and cuff,
he was used to the whitest of bread   35
and he fought bravely enough.

And two brothers joined this army,
each a mighty strategist,
these took an empty cottage by storm
with nothing but rain to resist.   40

And a lean grey fellow walked there,
by the roadside, in isolation,
and bore the burden of terrible guilt:
he came from a Nazi legation.

There was a musician among them   45
who in a shelled village found a drum one day
and was not allowed to strike it,
so as not to give them away.

And there was also a dog,
caught for the knife at the start,   50
yet later kept on as an eater
because no one had the heart.

And they had a school there also,
and a small teacher who knew how to yell,
and a pupil against the wall of a shot-up tank   55
as far as peac . . . learned to spell.

And there was a concert too:
by a roaring winter stream one lad
was allowed to beat the drum,
But no one heard him. Too bad.   60

And there was a love affair.
She was twelve, he was fifteen.
In a secluded courtyard
she combed his hair.

This love could not last long,   65
too cold the weather came on.
How can the little tree flower
with so much snow coming down?

And there was a war as well,
for there was another crowd beside this   70
and the war only came to an end
because it was meaningless.

But when the war still raged,
around a shelled pointsman's hut,
suddenly, so they say, one party   75
found their food supply had been cut.

And when the other heard this, they sent
a man to relieve their plight
with a sack of potatoes, because
without food one cannot fight.   80

strategist *somebody skilled in planning.*

legation *people in charge.*

pointsman *one in charge of points on railway.*

plight *difficult or unpleasant situation.*

110

There was a trial too,
with a pair of candles for light,
and after much painful examining
the judge was found guilty that night.

And a funeral too: of a boy   *85*
with velvet on collar and wrist;
it was two Poles and two Germans
carried him to his rest.

Protestant, Catholic and Nazi were there
when his body to earth they were giving,   *90*
and at the end a little Socialist spoke
of the future of the living.

So there was faith and hope,
only no meat and no bread,
and let no man blame them if they stole a few things   *95*
when he offered no board or bed.

And let no man blame the needy man
who offered no bread or rice,
for with fifty to feed it's a matter
of flour, not self-sacrifice.   *100*

They made for the south in the main.
The south is where the sun
at midday, twelve o'clock sharp
lies straight in front of one.

True, they found a soldier   *105*
who wounded on fir-needles lay.
They nursed him for seven days
so he could show them the way.

He told them: To Bilgoray!
Delirious, surely, far gone,   *110*   **delirious** *confused, semi-*
and he died on the eighth day.   *conscious.*
They buried him too, and moved on.

And there were sign-posts also,
though snow rubbed the writing out;
only they'd ceased to point the way,   *115*
having been turned about.

This was not for a practical joke,
but on a military ground,
and when they looked for Bilgoray
the place was not to be found.   *120*

They stood around their leader
who looked up at the snowy air
and, extending his little hand,
said, it must be over there.

112

Once, at night, they saw a fire,   125
but better not go, they decided.
Once three tanks rolled past them,
each with people inside it.

Once, too, they came to a city,
and skirted it, well out of sight;   130
till they'd left it well behind them
they only marched on at night.

In what used to be South-East Poland
when snow swept the landscape clean
that army of fifty-five children   135
was last seen.

If I close my eyes and try,
I can see them trudge on   *trudge* walk slowly and
from one shell-blasted homestead   *with difficulty.*
to another shell-blasted one.   140

Above them, in the cloudy spaces,
I see new long trains progress,
painfully trudging in the cold wind's face,
homeless, directionless.

Looking for the country at peace   145
without fire and thunder's blast,
not like that from which they have come;
and the train grows vast.

And soon in the flickering half-light
no longer the same it seemed: 150
other little faces I saw,
Spanish, French, yellow ones gleamed.

That January, in Poland
a stray dog was caught;
hanging from its lean neck   155
a cardboard notice it brought.

It read: please come and help us!
We no longer know the way.
There are fifty-five of us.
The dog won't lead you astray.   160   *astray* the wrong way.

Don't shoot him dead.
Only he knows the place
With him
our very last hope you'd efface.   *efface* destroy, obliterate.

The writing was in a child's hand.   165
By farmers it was read.
Since then a year and a half have passed.
The dog, who was starving, is dead.

☆   113

Assignments

○ *Poem in Performance*
In one large or several small groups, prepare a performance of this poem, suitable for presenting to an audience of younger children.

Begin by considering the audience: which details will need emphasising or omitting, to make the action clear to them?
Then decide how elaborate your performance will be and how long you will need to prepare it.
Will you arrange the poem for solo and groups of voices?
Will you attempt to act or mime some of the scenes?
Will you use costume, music, lighting, props?
To begin with, familiarise yourself with the poem by reading it through again as a group. A good way to do this is to read a line each, trying to keep the poem moving.
Look carefully at the punctuation – pause when you're told to, keep going if there's nothing to tell you to stop.

When you have read through the poem a few times, you will see that the story breaks down into a number of scenes. You may decide that one small group could be responsible for dramatising each scene. If you do this, set a deadline for when each group should have its scene ready for the performance.

Once you feel that you know the poem well, you may decide that you want to cut some lines and verses. If you decide to abridge the poem, make sure that what's left makes sense and flows smoothly.

You might like to turn the events of the poem into a play, either keeping Brecht's words, or providing your own. Try to give the main characters their own particular ways of talking.

○ *One Child's Account*
Write the diary of one of the fifty-five children in the crusade. Base your entries around the events narrated in the poem, but add plenty of details of your own.

○ *Newspaper or Radio Report*
Write an article for a local newspaper or prepare a radio documentary reporting the discovery of the dog and investigating various rumours surrounding the children's crusade. You might want to include interviews with people who remember seeing the children on their journey.

○ *Wall Frieze*
Try retelling the events of the poem through a series of pictures. You might work on this assignment as a group.

Some other poems which work well in performance

Robert Browning	*The Pied Piper of Hamelin*
Edward Lear	*The Jumblies; The Owl and the Pussy Cat; The Quangle Wangle Quee*
Samuel Taylor Coleridge	*The Ancient Mariner*
William Cowper	*The Diverting History of John Gilpin*
T.S. Eliot	*Macavity; Skimbleshanks*
Rudyard Kipling	*Danny Deever*

★

THE RESPONSIBILITY

Bob Dylan

MASTERS OF WAR

Owen

THE PARABLE OF THE OLD MEN
AND THE YOUNG

What do you understand by the word 'responsibility'?
Who do you think will be _responsible_ for what you do in the next ten years?
Yourself? Your parents, your teachers, your employers?
The government? The economy? The weather?
Luck? Fate? God?

When you were reading the poems written during the First World War, did
you get any sense of _why_ the war was being fought?
Who seemed to be in control of the men's destinies?
What seemed to be the attitude of the men to what was being done to them?

If there were another world war, who do you think would be responsible?
Us? The enemy? The soldiers? The generals? The manufacturers of weapons?
Destiny?

What point do you think this poet is making?

The Responsibility

I am the man who gives the word,
If it should come, to use the Bomb.

I am the man who spread the word
From him to them if it should come.

I am the man who gets the word   5
From him who spreads the word from him.

I am the man who drops the Bomb
If ordered by the one who's heard
From him who merely spreads the word
The first one gives if it should come.   10

I am the man who loads the Bomb
That he must drop should orders come
From him who gets the word passed on
By one who waits to hear from _him_.

I am the man who makes the Bomb   *15*
That he must load for him to drop
If told by one who gets the word
From one who passes it from *him.*

I am the man who fills the till,
Who pays the tax, who foots the bill   *20*
That guarantees the Bomb he makes
For him to load for him to drop
If orders come from one who gets
The word passed on to him by one
Who waits to hear it from the man   *25*
Who gives the word to use the Bomb.

I am the man behind it all;
I am the one responsible.

☆

How far do you agree with the poem's final line?

Here is another view:

Masters of War

Come you masters of war
You that build all the guns
You that build the death planes
You that build the big bombs
You that hide behind walls   *5*
You that hide behind desks
I just want you to know
I can see through your masks

You that never done nothin'
But build to destroy   *10*
You play with my world
Like it's your little toy
You put a gun in my hand
And you hide from my eyes
And you turn and run farther   *15*
When the fast bullets fly

Like Judas of old
You lie and deceive
A world war can be won
You want me to believe   *20*
But I see through your eyes
And I see through your brain
Like I see through the water
That runs down my drain

116

You fasten the triggers   *25*
For the others to fire
Then you set back and watch
When the death count gets higher
You hide in your mansion
As young people's blood   *30*
Flows out of their bodies
And is buried in the mud.

You've thrown the worst fear
That can ever be hurled
Fear to bring children   *35*
Into the world
For threatening my baby
Unborn and unnamed
You ain't worth the blood
That runs in your veins   *40*

How much do I know
To talk out of turn
You might say that I'm young
You might say I'm unlearned
But there's one thing I know   *45*
Though I'm younger than you
Even Jesus would never
Forgive what you do.

Let me ask you one question
Is your money that good   *50*
Will it buy you forgiveness
Do you think that it could
I think you will find
When your death takes its toll
All the money you made   *55*
Will never buy back your soul

And I hope that you die
And your death'll come soon
I will follow your casket
In the pale afternoon   *60*
And I'll watch while you're lowered
Down to your deathbed
And I'll stand o'er your grave
'Til I'm sure that you're dead.

☆

Thinking/Talking Points

▷ What seem to you the most important differences between the points of view of *The Responsibility* and *Masters of War*?

▷ What sort of 'masks' do you think the Masters of War wear?
Can you think of any recent example of behaviour similar to that described in the first three verses?

▷ Look again at stanza 4.
Behaviour is described but we are not given any *reasons* for it.
Can you suggest a motive for what is being done?

▷ Throughout the poem, the speaker uses very simple, direct language to discuss a complex and horrifying subject.
(a)   Why do you think he does that?
(b)   Do you think the style is effective?

▷ There is no compromise in the final verse:
'And I'll stand o'er your grave
'Til I'm sure that you're dead.'
Do you sympathise with that?
Who is in the coffin?

Here is a story from the Old Testament in the Bible.

> And it came to pass after these things, that God did tempt Abraham, and said unto him, "Abraham." And he said, "Behold, here I am." And he said, "Take now thy son, thine only son Isaac, whom thou lovest, and get thee into the land of Moriah; and offer him there for a burnt offering upon one of the mountains which I will tell thee of."
>
> And Abraham rose up early in the morning, and saddled his ass, and took two of his young men with him, and Isaac his son, and clave the wood for the burnt offering, and rose up, and went unto the place of which God had told him. Then on the third day Abraham lifted up his eyes, and saw the place afar off. And Abraham said unto his young men, "Abide ye here with the ass; and I and the lad will go yonder and worship, and come again to you." And Abraham took the wood of the burnt offering, and laid it upon Isaac his son; and he took the fire in his hand, and a knife; and they went both of them together. And Isaac spake unto Abraham his father and said, "My father." And he said, "Here am I, my son." And he said, "Behold the fire and the wood: but where is the lamb for a burnt offering?" And Abraham said, "My son, God will provide himself a lamb for a burnt offering." So they went both of them together.
>
> And they came to the place which God had told him of; and Abraham built an altar there, and laid the wood in order, and bound Isaac his son, and laid him on the altar upon the wood. And Abraham stretched forth his hand, and took the knife to slay his son. And the angel of the Lord called unto him out of heaven, and said, "Abraham. Abraham." And he said, "Here am I." And he said, "Lay not thine hand upon the lad, neither do thou any thing unto him: for now I know that thou fearest God, seeing thou hast not withheld thy son, thine only son from me." And Abraham lifted up his eyes, and looked, and behold behind him a ram caught in a thicket by his horns: and Abraham went and took the ram, and offered him up for a burnt offering in the stead of his son.
>
> *Genesis* 22, vv. 1–13

Here is Wilfred Owen's version of the story, written as a protest poem during the First World War.

The Parable of the Old Men and the Young

So Abram rose, and clave the wood, and went,　　　　　　　　*clave* cut.
And took the fire with him, and a knife.
And as they sojourned both of them together,　　　　　　　*sojourned* travelled.
Isaac the first-born spake and said, My Father,　　　　　　*spake* spoke.
Behold the preparations, fire and iron,　　　　　　　　5
But where the lamb for this burnt-offering?　　　　　　　*burnt-offering* sacrifice
　　　　　　　　　　　　　　　　　　　　　　　　　　made to a god.
Then Abram bound the youth with belts and straps,
And builded parapets and trenches there,　　　　　　　　*parapets* defensive walls of
And stretched forth the knife to slay his son,　　　　　　earth, stone or sandbags.
　　　　　　　　　　　　　　　　　　　　　　　　　　slay kill.
When lo! an angel called him out of heaven,　　　　　　10
Saying, Lay not thy hand upon the lad,
Neither do anything to him. Behold,
A ram, caught in a thicket by its horns;　　　　　　　　*thicket* undergrowth,
Offer the Ram of Pride instead of him.　　　　　　　　　bush.
But the old man would not so, but slew his son, –　　　15
And half the seed of Europe, one by one.　　　　　　　　*seed* children.

☆

Thinking/Talking Points

▷　What similarities is Owen suggesting between the Bible story and the First World War?

▷　What is the difference between Owen's version and the story in *Genesis*?

▷　What do you think is meant by 'the Ram of Pride'?
　　Why do you think Abram wouldn't sacrifice that instead of his son?

▷　What pictures does the final line of the poem suggest to you?

Assignments

○　Essay: *The Voice(s) of Protest*
　　Which of these three protest poems do you find most powerful? Do you find the views expressed echo your own? Are there things you would argue with in what the poems say?
　　Write about one (or all three) of the poems, saying what you most/least admire about it (or them) . . .

○　Write your own protest song or a fiery newspaper editorial drawing public attention to a particular evil in today's world (e.g. being protected by an arsenal of weapons sufficient to destroy the world; half the world starving whilst the other half makes itself ill by over-eating; animals being abused so we can have yet another lipstick or perfume).
　　You may like to create some characters like Dylan's Masters of War or Owen's Abram who stand for the evils and abuses which worry and anger you.

★

Have you ever witnessed an accident? Or seen somebody suddenly taken ill? What details can you remember?

How did the people around you react and behave?

What were your feelings? Did you want to turn away or go and see what was happening?

Read through this poem carefully a couple of times and then consider the points which follow.

At Bridlington Priory

She hurried slowly from neat bedsit to favourite pew,
While above her bells chimed the birth she came to hail.
Age chalked her face, only her stick gave sinew

But winter sun graced her, made our brief passing bright
In memory. It was a day of gold and blue, of light,   5
Of lawns and twigs, and wind in priory trees.

Held by beauty we sorted gloves, lingering.
Suddenly near us a boy and man were running.
Others were running, to gawp beside a heap of clothes.

The usual crowd gathered. In tribute the bells were stilled   10
– Their silence was terrible. A coat was spread
To hide the indecency of death, then, others more skilled

In such matters appearing (and having children's dreams
To consider) we turned aside to welcome Christmas Day.
Afterwards the Close was neat, all relics cleared away.   15

Priory bells rang once more, a verger shook hands, breath
Hung white against ancient stone, but still I saw Death
Shaped by a borrowed coat. That old woman's ending

Had become my question, my unease. Did she falling,
Die, or dying fall? And what if our passing   20
Were the jolt feeble foot and eye could not withstand?

All through the day doubt glanced between sunlit woman
And running man. Now, Pilate-like I wish she had chosen
Another death – or I had looked another way.

priory a religious house.

pew seat in church.
the birth she came to hail it was Christmas Day.
sinew strength.

graced made her beautiful.

gawp stare rudely.

Close area around the Priory.
relics reminders.

verger church caretaker.

Pilate-like like the Roman governor who didn't want to order the death of Jesus.

☆

Thinking/Talking Points

▷ Jot down a few words of your own to describe the woman as she is presented to us in the opening two stanzas.
What do you think the poet means when she says the woman 'hurried slowly'?

▷ Look again at stanza 2.
How do you picture this Christmas Day?

▷ Why do you think 'The usual crowd' gather round the dead woman?
What does the poet mean by 'the indecency of death'?

▷ What do you understand by: '. . . (and having children's dreams/To consider)'?

▷ Read stanzas 7 and 8 again.
Try to express in your own words the thoughts that are passing through the speaker's mind here.

Assignments

○ Write a poem or a short story, perhaps based upon personal experience, about an accident in which somebody is killed. Concentrate upon your own mixture of feelings and your observations of the way various people around you react.

○ Essay: *The Indecency of Death*
A hundred years ago, people were much more familiar with death than we are now. Without good food, warm housing and antibiotics, pneumonia and even 'flu were killers and many people died before reaching middle age. Many men died in accidents at work, many women in childbirth.
But that wasn't the only reason why people were more familiar with dying than we seem to be. When somebody died a hundred years ago, there was far more public awareness of the death: the curtains of the house would be drawn, the funeral procession might be very elaborate and the family would wear mourning (black clothes) for many months afterwards. Grief was something to be shown and shared.
Nowadays mourning has almost entirely disappeared and dying is simply not a subject many people are prepared to talk about.
Why do you think our attitude to death has become so fearful? So embarrassed?

○ Write about any experience you have had of death: either the death of somebody you were close to or a death you heard about in the news.
How did people around you react to the death? What did they say about it? Did they seem sad, frightened, anxious or indifferent? See if you can describe your own mixture of feelings. How do you think you were expected to behave? Was that difficult?
Do you think it is true that we regard the subject as too ugly to think about? Do you think that is a healthy thing?

Some further reading

Mary Lavin   *The Living* (short story)
Sylvia Plath   *Aftermath* (poem)
Susan Hill   *In The Springtime of the Year* (novel)

★

Dylan
WHO KILLED DAVEY MOORE?

Read through this song two or three times and then consider the points which
follow.

Who Killed Davey Moore?

Who killed Davey Moore,
Why an' what's the reason for?

'Not I,' says the referee,
'Don't point your finger at me.
I could've stopped it in the eighth   5
An' maybe kept him from his fate,
But the crowd would've booed, I'm sure,
At not gettin' their money's worth.
It's too bad he had to go,
But there was pressure on me too, you know   10
It wasn't me that made him fall.
No, you can't blame me at all.'

Who killed Davey Moore,
Why an' what's the reason for?

'Not us,' says the angry crowd,   15
Whose screams filled the arena loud.
'It's too bad he died that night
But we just like to see a fight.
We didn't mean for him t'meet his death,
We just meant to see some sweat,   20
There ain't nothing wrong in that.
It wasn't us that made him fall.
No, you can't blame us at all.'

Who killed Davey Moore,
Why an' what's the reason for?   25

'Not me,' says his manager,
Puffing on a big cigar.
'It's hard to say, it's hard to tell,
I always thought that he was well.
It's too bad for his wife an' kids he's dead,   30
But if he was sick, he should've said.
It wasn't me that made him fall.
No, you can't blame me at all.'

Who killed Davey Moore,
Why an' what's the reason for?   35

'Not me,' says the gambling man,
With his ticket stub still in his hand.
'It wasn't me that knocked him down,
My hands never touched him none.
I didn't commit no ugly sin,   40
Anyway, I put money on him to win.
It wasn't me that made him fall.
No, you can't blame me at all.'

Who killed Davey Moore,
Why an' what's the reason for?   45

'Not me,' says the boxing writer,
Pounding print on his old typewriter,
Sayin', 'Boxing ain't to blame,
There's just as much danger in a football game,'
Sayin', 'Fist fighting is here to stay,   50
It's just the old American way.
It wasn't me that made him fall.
No, you can't blame me at all.'

Who killed Davey Moore,
Why an' what's the reason for?   55

'Not me,' says the man whose fists
Laid him low in a cloud of mist,
Who came here from Cuba's door
Where boxing ain't allowed no more.
'I hit him, yes, it's true,   60
But that's what I am paid to do.
Don't say "murder," don't say "kill."
It was destiny, it was God's will.'

Who killed Davey Moore,
Why an' what's the reason for?   65

☆

Thinking/Talking Points

▷   Who killed Davey Moore?
    What blame do you think each of the following must accept for his death:
    (a) the referee   (b) the crowd   (c) the manager   (d) the gambler
    (e) the journalist   (f) the other boxer.

▷   Do you think anyone/anything else is accused in the poem?
    Is there anyone else you would charge with the murder?

▷   Why do you think boxing but not dog-fighting is still permitted by law?

Assignments

○   You may tackle this assignment singly or in a small group.
    The Big Fight
    (a)   Write the journalist's account of this fight. Imagine you are writing for a
          popular newspaper.
    (b)   Write an account of the fight from the point of view of one of the crowd
          who has money on Davey Moore.
    (c)   Write an account of the fight from the point of view of Davey's wife,
          listening to the fight on the radio.
    (d)   Write an account of the fight from the point of view of a witness who feels
          that boxing should be prohibited.

○   Essay: *Do you think boxing can be defended as a sport?*
    Boxing is the only sport in which people are allowed to strike at the
    unprotected head.
    Boxing is still an established feature of the Olympic Games.
    You may like to collect some information about the state of boxing today. e.g.
    How many people watched the last world championship? How much money
    changed hands in betting on the fight? What share of the 'purse' did the boxers
    end up with? What is the current thinking of doctors about the risks boxers
    take?
    Which voices are loudest in defence of the sport?
    How many boxers have died or been disabled by their boxing injuries in the last
    twenty years?

★

AUTOBAHNMOTORWAYAUTOROUTE

If a stranger watched the behaviour of your family or your group of friends, would there be anything which would strike him/her as funny?

Think about things people do every day which someone from another country might find ridiculous or odd.

What about a visitor from a far-off planet looking down upon the Earth? What human behaviour do you think he/she/it would find silliest or most difficult to understand?

Read through this poem a couple of times before considering the points which follow.

Autobahnmotorwayautoroute

Around the gleaming map of Europe
A gigantic wedding ring
Slowly revolves through Londonoslowestberlin
Athensromemadridparis and home again,
Slowly revolving.   5

That's no ring,
It's the Great European Limousine,
The Famous Goldenwhite Circular Car

Slowly revolving

All the cars in Europe have been welded together   10
Into a mortal unity,
A roundaboutgrandtourroundabout
Trafficjamroundaboutagain,
All the cars melted together,
Citroenjaguarbugattivolkswagenporschedaf.   15

Each passenger, lugging his
Colourpiano, frozenmagazines, high-fidog,
Clambers over the seat in front of him
Towards what looks like the front of the car.
They are dragging behind them   20
Worksofart, lampshades made of human money,
Instant children and exploding clocks.

But the car's a circle
No front no back
No driver no steering wheel no windscreen no brakes no   25

revolves goes round in a circle.

limousine a large, luxurious car.

lugging carrying with difficulty.

Thinking/Talking Points

▷ Can you explain the poem's title?
Why do you think it's written like that?

▷ What do you think each of the bits of luggage described in stanza 5 is like?
What's the poet saying about our habits?
Invent some extra items for the list.

▷ Read the last three lines of the poem again.
What do you think has happened to the cars?
Who's in control of the Great European Limousine?

▷ Do you think the poem has serious points to make? If so, what?

Assignments

○ Produce some illustrations for the poem.

○ Compose your own
Nineteeninineties' Blues/Calypso/Dirge/Jingle/Rock/Rap.
Decide first on what aspect(s) of our world you regard as crazy.
Then think about what would happen if something we do now were carried to ridiculous/dangerous extremes. (e.g. If everyone had wall-to-wall television; all food were man-made; fashions changed every day at noon; everything were taxed and all the taxes spent on weapons; old age were made illegal; computers ruled; etc.).

Some further reading

Gordon Dickson *Computers Don't Argue*
Ray Bradbury *Fahrenheit 451*

★

THE HUNCHBACK
IN THE PARK

What picture(s) does the title of this poem suggest to you?

Can you remember seeing a tramp and wondering about his lifestyle, his thoughts, his past?
What might be some of the reasons why people become down-and-outs?
Do you think you could survive, utterly alone?

In a radio broadcast called 'Reminiscences of Childhood', Dylan Thomas recalled the park he'd played in as a child:

> We knew every inhabitant of that park; every regular visitor; every nursemaid; every gardener; every old man. We knew the hour when the alarming retired policeman came in to look at the dahlias and the hour when the old lady arrived in the bath-chair with six pekinese, and a pale girl to read aloud to her. I think she read the newspaper, but we always said she read the *Wizard*. The face of the old man who sat summer and winter on the bench looking over the reservoir, I can see clearly now and I wrote a poem long after I'd left the park and the sea-town called: *The Hunchback in the Park*.

The Hunchback in the Park

The hunchback in the park
A solitary mister
Propped between trees and water
From the opening of the garden lock
That lets the trees and water enter   5
Until the Sunday sombre bell at dark   **sombre** *sad, mournful, gloomy.*

Eating bread from a newspaper
Drinking water from the chained cup
That the children filled with gravel
In the fountain basin where I sailed my ship   10
Slept at night in a dog kennel
But nobody chained him up.

Like the park birds he came early
Like the water he sat down
And Mister they called Hey Mister   15
The truant boys from the town
Running when he heard them clearly
On out of sound

Past lake and rockery
Laughing when he shook his paper 20
Hunchback in mockery
Through the loud zoo of the willow groves
Dodging the park keeper
With his stick that picked up leaves.

And the old dog sleeper 25
Alone between nurses and swans
While the boys among willows
Made the tigers jump out of their eyes
To roar on the rockery stones
And the groves were blue with sailors 30

Made all day until bell time
A woman figure without fault
Straight as a young elm
Straight and tall from his crooked bones
That she might stand in the night 35
After the locks and chains

All night in the unmade park
After the railings and shrubberies
The birds the grass the trees the lake
And the wild boys innocent as strawberries 40
Had followed the hunchback
To his kennel in the dark.

☆

from his crooked bones *in* Genesis *we are told that God created Eve from one of Adam's ribs.*

Thinking/Talking Points

▷ Look through the following list of words.
   Which would you use to describe the old man?
   Which details in the poem suggest them to you?
   friendly; familiar; isolated; despised; neglected; lonely; irritable; helpless;
   self-pitying; poor; imaginative; ugly; frightening; still; silent; proud; sad;
   humble.
   Add some words of your own to those you have chosen.

▷ What pictures does the second line of the poem suggest to you?

▷ What does the word 'propped' (line 3) imply about the old man?

▷ See if you can explain how
   ' . . . the opening of the garden lock
   . . . lets the trees and water enter'.

▷ Why do you think the poet describes the bell as
   'Sunday sombre'?

▷ Do you think it would have been *less* sad if someone *had* chained up the old
   man?

▷ Why do you think the poet describes the boys who torment the hunchback as
   'innocent as *strawberries*'?
   What do you imagine them doing when they
   'Made the tigers jump out of their eyes'?

▷ What do you associate with (a) nurses and (b) swans?
   What is the effect of this:
   'Alone between nurses and swans'?

▷ Look carefully at stanza 6.
   How might the hunchback *make* the woman?
   How do you imagine her?
   Read the poem again to see what other points need thinking about before you
   choose an assignment.

Assignments

○ As if you were filming him, write a description of the hunchback as he hears
   the bell, leaves the park and hobbles home.
   Add plenty of your own ideas to the details we're given in the poem.

○ Drawing on details from the poem but adding your own ideas, see if you can
   write a monologue (the hunchback's private thoughts), as he sits on his bench
   and reacts to what he sees and hears, remembers his past and dreams of his
   ideal companion.

○ Compose a character poem of your own, describing one of the following:
   a child waiting outside a pub; a junk man; a fortune-teller; a traveller; a down-
   and-out; a beachcomber; a knife-grinder; a busker; a circus performer; an old
   person in a wheelchair.

★

Masters
from SPOON RIVER ANTHOLOGY

Edgar Lee Masters's *Spoon River Anthology* was published in 1915. Like Dylan Thomas's play *Under Milk Wood* it is a portrait of a town and the people who live there. What the characters (they are actually all now ghosts) tell us about themselves and about one another is full of contradictions, slanders, half-truths and gossip.

Like real people, Masters's characters do not fully know themselves or one another. And they are not always honest about what they *do* know. The reader alone can begin to piece together some kind of truth about the town.

Here are a few of the colourful characters to give you a flavour of the anthology. Masters's work is as long as a parish register itself: 244 characters from 'Altman, Herman' to 'Zoll, Perry'.
We begin with the introduction to the anthology, *The Hill.*

from Spoon River Anthology
The Hill

WHERE are Elmer, Herman, Bert, Tom and Charley,
The weak of will, the strong of arm, the clown, the boozer,
                        the fighter?
All, all, are sleeping on the hill.

One passed in a fever,
One was burned in a mine,   5
One was killed in a brawl,
One died in a jail,
One fell from a bridge toiling for children and wife –
All, all are sleeping, sleeping, sleeping on the hill.

Where are Ella, Kate, Mag, Lizzie and Edith,   10
The tender heart, the simple soul, the loud, the proud,
                      the happy one? –
All, all, are sleeping on the hill.

One died in shameful child-birth,
One of a thwarted love,
One at the hands of a brute in a brothel,   15
One of a broken pride, in the search for heart's desire,
One after life in far-away London and Paris
Was brought to her little space by Ella and Kate and Mag –
All, all are sleeping, sleeping, sleeping on the hill.

thwarted *obstructed, unsuccessful.*

132

Where are Uncle Isaac and Aunt Emily,   20
And old Towny Kincaid and Sevigne Houghton,
And Major Walker who had talked
With venerable men of the revolution? –   *venerable* respected.
All, all, are sleeping on the hill.

They brought them dead sons from the war,   25
And daughters whom life had crushed,
And their children fatherless, crying –
All, all are sleeping, sleeping, sleeping on the hill.

Where is Old Fiddler Jones
Who played with life all his ninety years   30
Braving the sleet with bared breast,
Drinking, rioting, thinking neither of wife nor kin,
Nor gold, nor love, nor heaven?
Lo! he babbles of the fish-frys of long ago,
Of the horse-races of long ago at Clary's Grove,   35
Of what Abe Lincoln said
One time at Springfield.

☆

Here is a handful of the inhabitants, in their own words.
See how many of the 'facts' they present about themselves you are
able to cross-check.

Barney Hainsfeather

If the excursion train to Peoria   *excursion train* *train run*
Had just been wrecked, I might have escaped with my life –   *for special trips at reduced*
Certainly I should have escaped this place.   *rates.*
But as it was burned as well, they mistook me
For John Allen who was sent to the Hebrew Cemetery   5
At Chicago,
And John for me, so I lie here.
It was bad enough to run a clothing store in this town,
But to be buried here – *ach!*

Franklin Jones

If I could have lived another year
I could have finished my flying machine,
And become rich and famous.
Hence it is fitting the workman
Who tried to chisel a dove for me   5
Made it look more like a chicken.
For what is it all but being hatched,
And running about the yard,
To the day of the block?
Save that a man has an angel's brain,   10
And sees the ax from the first!

'Butch' Weldy

After I got religion and steadied down
They gave me a job in the canning works,
And every morning I had to fill
The tank in the yard with gasoline,
That fed the blow-fires in the sheds   5
To heat the soldering irons,
And I mounted a rickety ladder to do it,
Carrying buckets full of the stuff.
One morning, as I stood there pouring,
The air grew still and seemed to heave,   10
And I shot up as the tank exploded,
And down I came with both legs broken,
And my eyes burned crisp as a couple of eggs
For someone left a blow-fire going,
And something sucked the flame in the tank.   15
The Circuit Judge said whoever did it
Was a fellow-servant of mine, and so
Old Rhodes' son didn't have to pay me.
And I sat on the witness stand as blind
As Jack the Fiddler, saying over and over,   20
'I didn't know him at all.'

canning works factory where they put food into tins.
gasoline petrol.

circuit judge judge who travels round a particular district.

Blind Jack

I had fiddled all day at the county fair.
But driving home 'Butch' Weldy and Jack McGuire,
Who were roaring full, made me fiddle and fiddle
To the song of *Susie Skinner*, while whipping the horses
Till they ran away.   5
Blind as I was, I tried to get out
As the carriage fell in the ditch,
And was caught in the wheels and killed.
There's a blind man here with a brow
As big and white as a cloud.   10
And all we fiddlers, from highest to lowest,
Writers of music and tellers of stories,
Sit at his feet,
And hear him sing of the fall of Troy.

Lucius Atherton

When my moustache curled,
And my hair was black,
And I wore tight trousers
And a diamond stud,
I was an excellent knave of hearts and took many a trick.   5
But when the grey hairs began to appear —
Lo! a new generation of girls

Laughed at me, not fearing me,
And I had no more exciting adventures
Wherein I was all but shot for a heartless devil,   *10*
But only drabby affairs, warmed-over affairs
Of other days and other men.
And time went on until I lived at Mayer's restaurant,
Partaking of short-orders, a gray, untidy,
Toothless, discarded, rural Don Juan . . .   *15*
There is a mighty shade here who sings
Of one named Beatrice;
And I see now that the force that made him great
Drove me to the dregs of life.

The Town Marshal

The Prohibitionists made me Town Marshal

Prohibitionists *those who wanted a ban on alcohol.*

When the saloons were voted out,
Because when I was a drinking man,
Before I joined the church, I killed a Swede
At the saw-mill near Maple Grove.   *5*
And they wanted a terrible man,
Grim, righteous, strong, courageous,
And a hater of saloons and drinkers,
To keep law and order in the village.
And they presented me with a loaded cane   *10*
With which I struck Jack McGuire
Before he drew the gun with which he killed me.
The Prohibitionists spent their money in vain
To hang him, for in a dream
I appeared to one of the twelve jurymen   *15*
And told him the whole secret story.
Fourteen years were enough for killing me.

Judge Somers

How does it happen, tell me,
That I who was most erudite of lawyers,

erudite learned, scholarly.

Who knew Blackstone and Coke
Almost by heart, who made the greatest speech
The court-house ever heard, and wrote   *5*
A brief that won the praise of Justice Breese —
How does it happen, tell me,
That I lie here unmarked, forgotten,
While Chase Henry, the town drunkard,
Has a marble block, topped by an urn,   *10*

urn *large earthenware or metal vase for the ashes of the dead.*
***in a mood ironical** for a joke.*

Wherein Nature, in a mood ironical,
Has sown a flowering weed?

135

Chase Henry

In life I was the town drunkard;
When I died the priest denied me burial
In holy ground.
The which redounded to my good fortune.
For the Protestants bought his lot,   *5*
And buried my body here,
Close to the grave of the banker Nicholas,
And of his wife Priscilla.
Take note, ye prudent and pious souls,
Of the cross-currents in life   *10*
Which bring honor to the dead, who lived in shame.

Jack McGuire

They would have lynched me
Had I not been secretly hurried away
To the jail at Peoria.
And yet I was going peacefully home,
Carrying my jug, a little drunk,   *5*
When Logan, the marshal, halted me,
Called me a drunken hound and shook me,
And, when I cursed him for it, struck me
With that Prohibition loaded cane –
All this before I shot him.   *10*
They would have hanged me except for this:
My lawyer, Kinsey Keene, was helping to land
Old Thomas Rhodes for wrecking the bank,
And the judge was a friend of Rhodes
And wanted him to escape,   *15*
And Kinsey offered to quit on Rhodes
For fourteen years for me.
And the bargain was made. I served my time
And learned to read and write.

Doctor Meyers

No other man, unless it was Doc Hill
Did more for people in this town than I.
And all the weak, the halt, the improvident
And those who could not pay flocked to me.
I was good-hearted, easy Doctor Meyers.   *5*
I was healthy, happy, in comfortable fortune,
Blest with a congenial mate, my children raised,
All wedded, doing well in the world.
And then one night, Minerva, the poetess,
Came to me in her trouble, crying.   *10*

I tried to help her out – she died –
They indicted me, the newspapers disgraced me,
My wife perished of a broken heart.
And pneumonia finished me.

indicted me charged me
with the crime.

Minerva Jones

I am Minerva, the village poetess,
Hooted at, jeered at by the Yahoos of the street
For my heavy body, cock-eye, and rolling walk,
And all the more when 'Butch' Weldy
Captured me after a brutal hunt.   5
He left me to my fate with Doctor Meyers;
And I sank into death, growing numb from the feet up,
Like one stepping deeper and deeper into a stream of ice.
Will some one go the village newspaper,
And gather into a book the verses I wrote?–   10
I thirsted so for love!
I hungered so for life!

Yahoo brutish or bestial
person.
cock-eye squint.

Mrs Meyers

He protested all his life long
The newspapers lied about him villainously;
That he was not at fault for Minerva's fall,
But only tried to help her.
Poor soul so sunk in sin he could not see   5
That even trying to help her, as he called it,
He had broken the law human and divine.
Passers by, an ancient admonition to you:
If your ways would be ways of pleasantness,
And all your pathways peace,   10
Love God and keep his commandments.

admonition warning.

Lydia Puckett

Knowlt Hoheimer ran away to the war
The day before Curl Trenary
Swore out a warrant through Justice Arnett
For stealing hogs.
But that's not the reason he turned a soldier.   5
He caught me running with Lucius Atherton.
We quarreled and I told him never again
To cross my path.
Then he stole the hogs and went to the war –
Back of every soldier is a woman.   10

warrant document that
authorises arrest or police
search.

Assignment 1

○ Here are the names of some of the other characters in the *Spoon River Anthology*.
Use the names to write two or three portraits of your own in Masters's style:
Archibald Higbie; Mabel Osborne; Father Malloy; Magrady Graham;
Trainor the Druggist; Hildrup Tubbs; Ida Frickey; Dippold the Optician;
E.C. Culbertson.

○ Use one or two of the poems as the basis for a short story set in the town of
Spoon River.

    (a)   Decide on three or four episodes (adapted from the poems or wholly
invented) revolving about a central character.
Choose two or three other characters who will figure in those episodes.

    (b)   Add some biographical and descriptive details to what Masters gives us.

    (c)   Locate your story firmly: in the saloon, the schoolroom or in the
cemetery perhaps.

Try too to give some general impression of the atmosphere of the town.
You may write the story as an impersonal narrator or in the first person: i.e.
pretending to be one of the characters.

Assignment 2

○ Working as a group, produce your own *Anthology*.

    (a)   Decide on the town or village (perhaps your own) and the general
geography of the place. Where do people work and go to amuse
themselves?
Do different parts of the town have their own character?

    (b)   Next decide on your sample from the population, your Elmer, Herman,
Bert, Tom and Charley . . .
Who will typify the Respectable, the Layabout, the Hard-Working, the
Everybody's Girl, the Failure, Mrs Success, Mr Smooth, the Town's
Wiseman, the Fool . . . ? (Decide upon your own 'types'.)
You may decide (as Dylan Thomas did) that it's an unnecessary limitation
that all the characters should now be dead: people can reveal themselves
in dreams and daydreams too.

    (c)   Then produce a series of portraits.
Decide whether, like Masters, you want there to be commentary by one
character on another and if you wish to share any common themes
and/or events between the narratives, e.g. that fire at the school and who
was responsible; the business which is about to fold; the 'truth' about
Benny Jones's girlfriend . . .
Display your pieces, preferably illustrating them.

★

Acknowledgements

The author and publishers would like to thank the following for permission to reproduce copyright material.

'A Boy's Head' from *Selected Poems of Miroslav Holub* translated by Ian Milner and George Theiner (Penguin Modern European Poets, 1967), copyright © Miroslav Holub 1967, translation copyright © Penguin Books 1967, reproduced by permission of Penguin Books Ltd. 'Mirror' from *Crossing the Water* and 'Mushrooms' from *The Colossus* by Sylvia Plath, published by Faber and Faber Ltd, copyright Ted Hughes, reprinted by permission of Olwyn Hughes. 'Odd' from *Collected Poems 1948–1976* by Dannie Abse, published by Hutchinson and Co. Ltd. 'Children' from *Close Relatives* by Vicki Feaver, reprinted by permission of Martin Secker and Warburg Ltd. 'Song of the Wagon Driver' by B.S. Johnson, reprinted by permission of John Farquharson Ltd. 'A Constable Calls' from *North*, 'The Names of the Hare' from *The Rattle Bag*, An Advancement of Learning' and 'Dawn Shoot' from *Death of a Naturalist* by Seamus Heaney, reprinted by permission of Faber and Faber Ltd. 'The Burglary' from *New and Selected Poems* by Tony Connor, reprinted by permission of Anvil Press Poetry. 'The Highwayman' from *Collected Poems* by Alfred Noyes, reprinted by permission of John Murray (Publishers) Ltd. 'Considering the Snail' from *My Sad Captains* by Thom Gunn, reprinted by permission of Faber and Faber Ltd. 'First Blood' © Oxford University Press 1963, reprinted from *Out of Bounds* by Jon Stallworthy (1963) by permission of Oxford University Press. 'In Memory of God' by Jenny Joseph from *Beyond Descartes*, Secker and Warburg, 1983. 'Wind' from *Hawk in the Rain* by Ted Hughes, reprinted by permission of Faber and Faber Ltd. 'Flannan Isle' from *Collected Poems 1905–1925* by W.W. Gibson, reprinted by permission of Mr Michael Gibson and Macmillan, London and Basingstoke. Extract from *A Reader's Guide to G.M. Hopkins* by N. MacKenzie, reprinted by permission of Thames and Hudson Ltd. 'The Jewel Stairs' Grievance' and 'The River-Merchant's Wife: a Letter' from *Collected Shorter Poems* by Ezra Pound, reprinted by permission of Faber and Faber Ltd. 'Spacepoem 3' and 'First Men on Mercury' from *Poems of Thirty Years* by Edwin Morgan (1982), reprinted by permission of Carcanet Press Ltd. 'Bombardment' by Richard Aldington from *Men Who March Away* edited by Ian Parsons, reprinted by permission of the estate of the editor and Chatto and Windus. Extract from 'Fetching the Wounded' by Laurence Binyon, reprinted by permission of Mrs Nicolette Gray and the Society of Authors on behalf of the Laurence Binyon Estate. 'Children's Crusade 1939' from *Tales from the Calendar* by Bertolt Brecht, translated by Michael Hamburger, reprinted by permission of Methuen London. 'Masters of War' by Bob Dylan © 1963 Warner Bros. Inc. All rights reserved. Used by permission. 'Who Killed Davey Moore?' by Bob Dylan © 1964, 1965 Warner Bros. Inc. All rights reserved. Used by permission. 'At Bridlington Priory' by Pauline Kirk, reprinted from *Purple and Green* by permission of Rivelin Grapheme Press. 'Autobahnmotorwayautoroute' from *Ride the Nightmare* by Adrian Mitchell, reprinted by permission of Jonathan Cape Ltd. 'The Hunchback in the Park' from *The Poems* by Dylan Thomas, published by Dent. Selected poems from *Spoon River Anthology* by Edgar Lee Masters, reprinted by permission of Ellen. C. Masters.

Every effort has been made to reach copyright holders; the publishers would be glad to hear from anyone whose rights they have unknowingly infringed.

The authors and publishers would also like to thank the following for permission to reproduce photographs:

p.6 Steve Benbow. p.10 Andre Gelpke. p.35 © Charles Keeping 1981, from *The Highwayman* by Alfred Noyes, Oxford University Press. p.37 Graphische Sammlung Albertina, Vienna. p.41 Sotheby's. p.63 Fay Godwin's Photo Files. p.70 National Maritime Museum, London. p.91 The Tate Gallery, London. p.95 Iris Brosch. p.98 Rene Burri Magnum, by permission of News Productions. p.105 U.S. National Archives. p.111 Sandra Petrillo, by permission of News Productions. p.126 Tom Learmonth. p.129 Raymond Depardon, by permission of News Productions.

Published by the Press Syndicate of the University of Cambridge
The Pitt Building, Trumpington Street, Cambridge CB2 1RP
40 West 20th Street, New York, NY 10011–4211, USA
10 Stamford Road, Oakleigh, Melbourne 3166, Australia

First published 1989
Fifth printing 1996

Printed in Great Britain by Scotprint Ltd, Musselburgh, Scotland

British Library cataloguing in publication data

Wood, Lynn
Cambridge poetry workshop 14+
1. Poetry in English. Criticism – Questions
& answers – For schools
I. Title   II. Wood, Jeffrey
821'.0076

ISBN 0 521 33673 2

GO